D0205396

Neighborhoods, Family, and Political Behavior in Urban America

CONTEMPORARY URBAN AFFAIRS
VOLUME 3
GARLAND REFERENCE LIBRARY OF SOCIAL SCIENCE
VOLUME 1110

CONTEMPORARY URBAN AFFAIRS

RICHARD D. BINGHAM, *Series Editor*

Neighborhoods, Family, and Political Behavior in Urban America

Yvette M. Alex-Assensoh

The Maxine Goodman Levin College of Urban Affairs at Cleveland State University

THE URBAN CENTER

Garland Publishing, Inc.
A member of the Taylor & Francis Group
New York and London
1998

Library of Congress Cataloging-in-Publication Data

Alex-Assensoh, Yvette M.
    Neighborhoods, family, and political behavior in urban America /
Yvette M. Alex-Assensoh.
        p.   cm. — (Garland reference library of social science ; vol. 1110.
Contemporary urban affairs ; vol. 3)
    Includes bibliographical references and index.
    ISBN 0-8153-2381-6 (alk. paper)
    1. Urban poor—United States—Political activity.   2. Community
development, Urban—United States.   3. Marginality, Social—United
States.   4. Neighborhood—United States.   I. Title.   II. Series:
Garland reference library of social science. Contemporary urban affairs ;
vol. 3.
HV4045A75   1998
322.4'3'0869420973—dc21   98-5122
                                                                      CIP

Printed on acid-free, 250-year-life paper
Manufactured in the United States of America

For Kwadwo Stephen Alex Assensoh,
who is the precious fruit of an
everlasting bond of love.

Contents

Acknowledgments

I now agree that completing a book manuscript is neither an easy task nor the achievement of the individual author, hence there is need for me—at this juncture—to pause and express my gratitude to several individuals and institutions for their assistance in a variety of ways. First and foremost, I would like to thank the numerous scholars in the fields of urban politics, urban poverty, contextual analysis and political participation whose pioneering efforts and publications have laid an enduring and a very splendid foundation upon which my humble efforts in this publication are based.

Specifically, I owe an unlimited expression of gratitude to Herbert Asher, Aage Clausen, Paul Beck and William E. Nelson, Jr., my former professors at Ohio State University, who taught and ably guided me in the formative years of my graduate studies in political science, particularly as I endeavored to formulate the initial ideas for this work. Apart from sharing and imparting knowledge to my fellow classmates and me in the classroom, I also always remember their patience in listening to my persistent queries, coupled with my requests for extra time in their busy schedules so that I could delve deeper into specific topics in urban politics, urban poverty, contextual analysis and political participation.

Indeed, there were other organizations and scholars outside the Ohio State University intellectual scene, from whose circles and substantively helpful comments I benefitted a great deal. Promptly, I wish to underscore that I gained a lot from my early participation in the Harvard Conference on Race, Ethnicity and Governance, sponsored by Professor Paul Peterson of the Department of Government at Harvard University as well as the Social Science Research Council (SSRC)

Final Fellows' Conference on the Urban Underclass. Certainly, the intellectually charged comments of conference participants went a long way to enrich the theoretical framework of my study. Special word of gratitude is owed to Professors Hanes Walton, Jr., and Jeffrey Berry, who read the entire manuscript and offered extremely useful comments to help in improving the final product. I also gratefully acknowledge Professors Maurice Woodard, Jewel Prestage and Dr. Catherine Rudder who have played important roles in my professional development.

I am also greatly indebted to several organizations and foundations for their generous financial support that allowed me to conduct the initial but very crucial survey and the related interviews of neighborhood organizational leaders for the entire study: they include the National Science Foundation (NSF); Social Science Research Council (SSRC); Ford Foundation; Ohio State University Graduate Student Research Award; and Indiana University Small Grants Program. Also, some of the initial aspects of the manuscript for this publication were written during my one-year post-doctoral stint in the Political Science Department of the University of North Carolina (UNC) at Chapel Hill. For making my research affiliation with UNC a pleasant one, I am especially grateful to Professors David Lowery, George Rabinowitz, Stuart MacDonald and James Johnson. All of these scholars made themselves available to me in a variety of ways, especially Dr. Johnson, who has been associated with my research interests since his leadership years at UCLA, where I also had a summer pre-doctoral stint at the Urban Poverty Center, which was co-directed by Dr. Johnson and Dr. Melvin Oliver. Dr. Oliver, who also provided me with useful scholarly assistance, currently serves as Vice-President for Asset Building and Community Development at the Ford Foundation in New York. I am also grateful to my colleagues at Indiana University, who have provided a conducive environment for the production of this manuscript. Special gratitude is extended to Robert Huckfeldt, who provided scholarly encouragement as I completed the manuscript. I am also grateful to Christine Barbour and Jerry Wright, whose dinner parties provided a delightful respite from the pressures of the writing process as well as an enjoyable atmosphere for intellectual discourse.

Also, I am very grateful to the late Mrs. Mamie Flack and Ms. Toni Reddick of Columbus, Ohio, both of whom—as my fellow church members at the local Seventh Avenue Baptist Church—patiently as well as supportively drove with me up and down the streets of several

Columbus census tracts, particularly as I selected neighborhoods for the earlier study as well as the present one. Additionally, I am grateful to my parents, Rev. Livingston Alex and Mrs. Thelma Coleman Alex and other family members—including my godmother, Mrs. Enola Thomas, and Mrs. Etta Pearl Brew—for their continuous support in a variety of ways.

This publication would not have been completed as promptly as it was without the persistence and patient prodding of Professor Richard D. Bingham of Maxine Goodman Levin College of Urban Affairs at Cleveland State University, as the hard-working editor of the Contemporary Urban Affairs Series of Garland Publishing. His initial expert evaluation of the outline for this study as well as his willingness in reviewing subsequent manuscripts that I completed and promptly returning them to me with very useful and, sometimes, "soothing" comments, boosted my desire to complete this publication. In the end, it was also the constant contacts of Garland senior editor David Estrin— through e-mail, telephone and postal mail—that prompted me to work hard to live up to the publisher's deadline, which had been enshrined in the signed contract.

Above all, I feel extremely blessed to have a loving, understanding and very patient husband in Dr. A. B. Assensoh, a journalist and historian, who is a scholar in his own right. Affectionately called "A.B." by his colleagues, friends and students, my husband was always there for me as my "soul mate" as well as patiently serving as my sounding board whenever I needed someone, at odd hours of the day, to listen to some of my frustrations in research. Additionally, he appreciated and understood the bulk of time, effort and solitude that were very much necessary for the successful completion of a scholarly manuscript. I very much appreciated the fact that he selflessly took care of our infant son, Kwadwo, especially in handling the bulk of our household chores and also ran most of our family's errands as I grudgingly reclused myself in order to complete this book. On the intellectual plane, A.B. offered useful suggestions for the improvement of the histo-political aspects of the manuscript and, in the end, he offered the requisite encouragement that I often needed to reassure myself that, yes, this study was worth being brought to fruition in the sea of constant doubt and frustration. Forever, I am grateful to him, particularly for his unyielding and unconditional love!

Although many individuals and institutions have done a great deal to assist in bringing my research interests into fruition, within the context of this book, I still feel eternally responsible for any possible shortcomings or omissions that critics may detect in the final product.

Neighborhoods, Family, and Political Behavior in Urban America

CHAPTER 1

Introduction

> I am an invisible man . . . I am invisible, understand, simply because people refuse to see me. . . . When they approach me they see only my surroundings, themselves or figments of their imagination— indeed, everything and anything except me. (Ellison 1952, *Invisible Man*)

Over the last two decades, American society has witnessed dramatic increases in the growth of single-parent households and the emergence of concentrated poverty neighborhoods, where a minimum of 40% of the residents live below the poverty line. Studies have shown that the foregoing trends have appeared to converge in inner-city communities, where social isolation and antisocial behaviors are commonplace due to the lack of contact or sustained interaction with mainstream society (Wilson and Wacquant 1989; Mead 1992; Murray 1984; Lemann 1991; Jencks and Peterson 1991; Wilson 1987, 1996). These trends have led urban poverty scholars to argue that inner-city communities are beleaguered by a new kind of urban poverty which is more invidious, pervasive and debilitating than the impoverishment of the past (Wilson 1987, 1996).

In comparison to residents of working or middle-class neighborhoods, residents of many inner-city, concentrated poverty communities experience higher levels of criminal activity and joblessness and are more likely to be poorly educated (Kirschenman and Neckerman 1991; Anderson 1991; Crane 1991). In earlier decades, the poor frequently interacted with individuals and institutions in the economic and social mainstreams. In contrast, today's impoverished inner-city residents are socially and spatially isolated from mainstream

America, making it almost impossible to traverse the barriers of the new urban ghettos (Wilson and Wacquant 1989; Massey and Denton 1993). Many individuals in contemporary urban ghettos are poor, chronically unemployed, welfare dependent, ill-housed and poorly educated; however, they are invisible in the eyes of policy-makers, political candidates and employers—very similar to the plight that Richard Wright bemoaned in the opening quotation.

In many respects, the current social contexts of contemporary inner-city communities not only damage the social, economic and psychological well being of urban areas, but they also threaten the norms of political stability and democracy in America. After all, political participation is important because it serves as a vehicle for the transmission of public opinion and policy preferences (Verba and Nie 1972; Verba, Schlozman and Brady 1995; Walton 1985). As a democracy, America's governmental process is rooted in the belief that all citizens are equally endowed with the ability to access the policy-making process (Dahl 1961). Historically, disenfranchised and disfranchised groups have utilized the political system to redress past grievances as evinced in the Civil Rights movement and the election of political officials who improved the public services of formerly disenfranchised citizens (Button 1989; Morris 1984). However, if inner-city residents by virtue of being embedded in debilitating social contexts are isolated from the policy process, political networks and institutions, then the American ideal of participatory democracy is threatened.

Therefore, the overall purpose of this book is to examine the political consequences of today's urban social context including concentrated poverty neighborhoods and single-parent household structures on the political behavior of white and black inner-city residents. In this respect, it builds on the ground-breaking work of Cohen and Dawson, which examined the effects of concentrated poverty neighborhoods on the political behavior of African American inner-city residents (Cohen and Dawson 1993). Additionally, the study examines whether or not the social context of inner-city communities impedes access to politically relevant resources which play an important role in facilitating political participation. The remaining sections of Chapter One provide a thematic context for the study by offering an overview of the urban poverty debate and the research on urban political behavior.

THE ORIGINS OF THE NEW URBAN POVERTY

Although cities have historically been recognized as the wellspring of American economic power, they have invariably wrestled with the social consequences of economic processes and transformations in the absence of formidable and ameliorative political power (Judd 1988; Judd and Kantor 1992; Stone 1987). In the wake of America's industrial revolution, the fledgling nineteenth-century urban political institutions were no match for the problems of immigration, ethnic conflict, inadequate housing and socio-economic disorder that beleaguered early American cities until the enactment of ameliorative federal urban policy in the late 1930s.[1] Under President Franklin Delano Roosevelt's leadership, America embarked on a four-decade-long federal-urban partnership, which recognized the economic importance of cities and addressed urban policy from a federal perspective, a trend which predominated until the late 1970s.

Economic restructuring of the mid-1970s and 1980s, however, once again transformed the social and political landscape of American cities. The decline and decentralization of inner-city manufacturing jobs, coupled with the rise of low-wage service sector employment, significantly reduced the number of low-skilled jobs that paid a living wage (Kasarda 1985). The resulting high rate of joblessness in inner-city America was exacerbated by middle-class and white flight to the suburbs. This exodus occurred alongside a decline in public services and private investment. These trends magnified problems of income inequality as well as racial and class segregation in housing and educational facilities (Massey and Denton 1993; Orfield and Ashkinaze 1991).

Unlike previous decades of urban social dislocation wherein the federal government enacted ameliorative policy, the 1980 administration of Ronald Reagan considered inner-city communities a necessary casualty of the economic and technological revitalization of America. The urban distress, resulting from redistributions of the population and economic activity, was rationalized as a necessary part of America's economic renewal (Warren 1995). In many American cities, the political power of municipal governments and urban residents became subordinated to the power and benefits of the market as well as the whims and caprices of private firms, corporations and the logic of growth politics. This historical problem has left cities vulnerable to the frequently devastating social consequences of economic changes and processes.

Among the most serious consequences of the foregoing technological revolution and economic restructuring is the seemingly intractable problem of inter-generational poverty and chronic joblessness that resulted for millions of urban Americans, but especially for inner-city residents in northern and midwestern cities. While poverty and ghettos have been permanent features of American life, today's genre of urban poverty is more intransigent, the ghettos are more isolated and its inhabitants are much less hopeful of moving beyond the pale of inner-city poverty (Warren 1995; Kotlowitz 1991; Massey and Denton 1993; Wilson 1996). Immigrant ghettos of the past were bearable in the sense that they were transitional residences, the proverbial stepping stones to a better life (Handlin 1973; Muller 1993). Moreover, residents of earlier urban ghettos were often connected to more prosperous and progressive relatives who were integrated into the mainstream of society (Massey and Denton 1993). In contrast, contemporary urban ghettos are much more spatially isolated and their residents experience a social isolation that is far greater than that of the past. These ghettos are commonly described as a "no man's land" filled with abandoned and boarded-up commercial buildings, dilapidated housing, vacant lots, abandoned cars and an ever-growing population of people who fall below the poverty line and are chronically unemployed (Wilson 1987, 1996; Anderson 1989).

Over the last two decades, there has been an unrelenting increase in the growth of spatially isolated, concentrated poverty neighborhoods, a precipitous rise in single-parent households, and the increased estrangement of inner-city residents from the American mainstream (Jargowsky and Bane 1991; Green 1990, 1991; Mincy, Sawhill and Wolf 1990; Wilson 1980, 1987; Wilson and Wacquant 1989). Social scientists and journalists initially utilized the term "underclass" to describe individuals who were affected by the foregoing socio-economic transitions and were consequently chronically jobless, unable to take care of themselves and their families and who were predisposed to antisocial and criminal behaviors.

WHAT IS THE URBAN "UNDERCLASS" ?

In many respects, the term "underclass" has taken on a variety of different meanings and connotations since Myrdal first utilized it in

1963 to describe individuals who were cut off from the labor market (Myrdal 1963). William Julius Wilson later defined the term urban "underclass" to include descriptions of status as well as behavior. According to Wilson, the "underclass" consists of "individuals who lack training, skills and either suffer from long-term unemployment or are not part of the labor force . . . who are engaged in street crime and other forms of aberrant behavior" (Wilson 1987). Others focused primarily on behavioral characteristics by arguing that the underclass consists of individuals who fall into the following four categories: long-term welfare recipients, violent street crime offenders, non-violent hustlers and the mentally ill (Auletta 1982). Some scholars have intentionally derived definitions of the "underclass" that are antonyms for middle-class behavior in arguing that the "underclass" is best defined by chronic joblessness and the lack of a commitment to mainstream values (Jencks 1991).

Meanwhile, other social scientists have contended that it is important to remember the multi-dimensional and contextual aspects of the "underclass" phenomenon. Johnson and Oliver have warned against defining the "underclass" solely in terms of behavioral tendencies because it is possible to be jobless and a resident of ghetto neighborhoods without necessarily exhibiting such so-called "underclass" behaviors as out-of-wedlock births, family disruption, criminal activity and long-term welfare dependency (Johnson and Oliver 1991). Van Haitsma has argued that definitions of the urban "underclass" should be embedded in specific social contexts. As a result, her proposed definition of the underclass includes "those persons who are weakly connected with the formal labor force and whose social context tends to maintain or further weaken this attachment" (Van Haitsma 1990).

Operationalizations for the "underclass" concept as well as the use of the term "underclass" have also been the subject of an extensive debate and scrutiny. Consequently, operationalizations of the "underclass" concept range from concentration of individuals who fall below the poverty line (Jargowsky and Bane 1991) to geographic concentration of aberrant behaviors (Ricketts and Sawhill 1988) and persistence of poverty and weak labor force attachment (Tienda and Stier 1991; Van Haitsma 1990).

FROM "UNDERCLASS" TO ESTRANGED POOR

Initially, skepticism over the use of the "underclass" concept revolved around the lack of a lucid and acceptable meaning of the term. In a thought-provoking essay about the urban "underclass," Adolph Reed, Jr. argues that the term "underclass" is a powerful metaphor with very little empirical and substantive content (Reed 1991). Others argue that the term contributes to the "blaming the victim" mentality, which often stalls debate about policy issues (Abramowitz 1992), while still others maintain the term is ambiguous because it is utilized outside the historical-political framework of substantive meaning (Katz 1993). Recent criticisms of the term, however, highlight its stigmatizing nature, and Wilson, who is responsible for its revival, has subsequently recommended that social scientists refrain from using the term.

One political scientist has maintained that analyses of the so-called urban underclass have devoted more attention to the cultural and moral dimensions without adequate attention to the role of economics (Henry 1992). He continues by noting that analyses of the underclass should focus more attention on the diversity among the impoverished and their relationship to the broader political and economic institutions (Henry 1992). Some researchers have subsequently relied upon such terms as the "ghetto poor" (Wilson and Wacquant 1989) to describe individuals and "concentrated poverty neighborhoods" or "ghetto poor" or "estranged poor neighborhoods" (Hochschild 1989) to refer to their communities. This study will utilize the terms "chronically impoverished" or "ghetto poor" to describe the population that is commonly referred to as the "underclass." However, it is important to underscore that the study is less concerned about terminology than ascertaining the political consequences of concentrated poverty neighborhoods, social isolation and single-parent households for white and black inner-city residents. Toward that end, it is necessary to understand the diverse explanations that have been offered to explain the emergence and proliferation of contemporary poverty in inner-city America.

CULTURAL EXPLANATIONS FOR CONTEMPORARY URBAN POVERTY

A variety of explanations have been set forth to explain the emergence of the modern-day ghettos and the so-called underclass. In many respects, the modern urban poverty debate began with the publication of Charles Murray's *Losing Ground,* which attempted to explain the growing problems of poverty in inner-city America in general and among African Americans in particular (Murray 1984). According to Murray, liberal social policies had changed the incentive structure for work and made it more profitable to remain on the public dole than to work for a living. Instead of helping the poor, Murray argued that social welfare policies had facilitated a culture of poverty-cum-dependence, which—in his opinion—reinforced deviant values that were at odds with American work ethics and civic virtues. In Murray's estimation, a culture of dependence on welfare benefits had given rise to criminal behavior and skyrocketing illegitimacy that ravaged inner-city communities. Murray advocated a sharp reduction in the size of government as well as social welfare programs. Unchallenged by liberal and moderate academics, the Murray thesis was reportedly utilized in the 1980s as a rationale for the massive cuts in federal social welfare spending.

Following Murray's conservative lead was Lawrence Mead, who argued that the plight of extremely poor minorities in inner-city communities was the result of a culture of dependence facilitated by government social programs. According to Mead, inner-city residents had lost the desire and capacity to work and function as ordinary citizens. In contrast to Murray's call for less government, Mead issued an alternative proposition of a paternalistic and authoritarian government, whereby individuals would be made to work regardless of the conditions or level of remuneration (Mead 1986).

In many respects, a key aspect of earlier analyses by Murray and others rested on the proposition that welfare dependency was the central causal factor. According to these analysts, dependence on welfare benefits was responsible for social problems ranging from out-of-wedlock births to intergenerational poverty and socially disintegrating communities (Auletta 1982; Loury 1985; Murray 1984).

While the Mead and Murray theses implicitly discussed the culture of poverty as an explanation of underclass phenomenon, Nicholas Lemann's work on the urban underclass explicitly sets forth a culture of poverty explanation. Lemann has underscored further that "every aspect of the underclass culture in the ghettos is directly traceable to roots in the South and not the South of Slavery, but the South of a generation ago . . . the nascent underclass of the sharecropper South" (Lemann 1986a). In Lemann's estimation, the behavioral characteristics of the urban underclass like illegitimacy, dependency, poverty, crime and lack of education were brought to the north by southern sharecroppers (Lemann 1986a). According to Lemann, amelioration of the so-called underclass problems will only prevail when public policy imposes a more disciplined culture on the lives of inner-city residents.

STRUCTURAL EXPLANATIONS FOR THE NEW URBAN POVERTY

The major liberal response to the culture-centered and conservative theories of urban poverty was William Julius Wilson's *The Truly Disadvantaged*. According to Wilson, the current manifestations of urban poverty were not a result of social welfare policy (Murray 1984), unwillingness to work (Mead 1986), or a culture of poverty (Lemann 1991), but rather the result of economic restructuring and migration patterns which left poorly skilled inner-city blacks jobless and socially isolated from the mainstream of America. In revitalizing the "underclass" concept, Wilson further argued that the so-called pathologies of illegitimacy, single-parent households, crime and high drop-out rates that plagued communities were not a result of cultural predispositions or welfare dependence but the consequences of living in spatially and socially isolated concentrated poverty neighborhoods that were devoid of legitimate social and political institutions and networks. Men were unable to find jobs, the pool of marriageable partners declined while out-of-wedlock births and female-headed households increased (Wilson 1987; Wilson and Wacquant 1989; Kasarda 1989). According to Wilson, blacks were the most susceptible to these structural changes because they were concentrated in inner-city communities where economic restructuring was the most profound.

Other scholars have argued that Wilson's focus on concentrated poverty neighborhoods is misguided because concentrated poverty neighborhoods are not a new American phenomenon (Massey and Denton 1993). Rather, the concentration of poor individuals was even more problematic during the 1930s. In contrast, the team of Massey and Denton argues that the scourge of poverty and social isolation in American inner-city communities is the result of an interaction between the poverty level and the historical-cum-contemporary patterns of residential segregation that blacks have endured. Using careful historical analysis, Massey and Denton argue that the racial segregation of American cities is responsible for the current problems of concentrated poverty neighborhoods. In turn, racial segregation is the result of a complex web of forces including restrictive covenants, redlining by banks and insurance companies, zoning, corrupt practices by some real estate agents and the creation of public housing projects in low-income areas (Massey and Denton 1993).

While Wilson and the team of Massey and Denton differ in their identification of the root causes of urban poverty, they agree on the consequences of such debilitating neighborhood environments in facilitating social isolation among inner-city residents, which disconnects them from social, economic, marital and political networks.

Other scholars have echoed Wilson as well as Massey and Denton's focus on structural forces and emphasized the historical importance of racial discrimination in the economic arena (Jones 1992; Henry 1992), as well as the negative prejudicial role of white attitudes, limited employment opportunities and social mobility of inner-city minorities (Kirschenman and Neckerman 1991; Braddock and McPartland 1987).

Still others have forcefully argued that the underclass is not new but a contemporary manifestation of an enduring legacy of racial discrimination. The underlying thesis of these analyses posited that the underclass is a systemic and natural outcome of racial discrimination that is perpetuated by American social, economic and political institutions, and that the underclass will cease to exist only when America rectifies its system of racial inequity through the development of black political power (Jones 1992; Jennings 1992a).

The debate between structural and cultural theorists has spawned an expansive literature about the causes, influences and consequences of persistent and concentrated urban poverty. Researchers have investigated the respective effects of residence in concentrated poverty neighborhoods and single-parent households on educational attainment (Crane 1991; Mayer 1991), welfare dependence (Bane and Ellwood 1994; Murray 1984), illegitimacy (Anderson 1989, 1991; Mare and Winship 1991), criminal behavior (Greenstone 1991), and employment (Freeman 1991; Osterman 1991; Tienda and Stier 1991; Kirschenman and Neckerman 1991). Limitations in the literature are evident on two fronts. First, the urban poverty literature frequently characterizes the problems of urban America in racially specific terms, but there is very little empirical research on the similarities and differences experienced by whites and blacks in inner-city contexts. Second, there is very little information on the consequences of concentrated poverty neighborhoods, single-parent households and social isolation for political behavior.

RACE AND URBAN POVERTY

The urban poverty debate is characterized by the lack of empirical evidence about the role that race plays in the emergence and maintenance of contemporary urban poverty. The prevalent view held by both academics and policy makers is that underclass behaviors are predominantly characteristic of African American communities. However, more recent studies that are based on the 1990 census suggest that the underclass phenomenon has diffused down the urban hierarchy to small and medium-sized cities (Pear 1993). These findings are in keeping with an earlier study that showed that concentrated poverty neighborhoods dominated by whites are often overlooked because of a focus on large cities (Mincy 1988). Subsequent studies have shown that the largest increase in concentrated poverty neighborhoods occurred among non-Hispanic whites (141%), while the number of non-Hispanic black neighborhoods increased by only 49% (Mincy and Wiener 1995). This pattern is in direct contrast to that of the 1970s when the growth in concentrated poverty communities occurred primarily among African Americans in large communities (Wilson 1987; Jencks and Peterson 1991). The growth in concentrated poverty neighborhoods dominated by whites presents a perfect opportunity to examine the extent to which anti-social behaviors associated with the African American inner-city communities are race-specific. Moreover, it presents an opportunity to examine the political consequences of racial-cum-class segregation on the political behavior of blacks and whites in similar contextual environments.

POLITICAL CONSEQUENCES: THE MISSING FACTOR IN URBAN POVERTY RESEARCH

There is a rich base of anthropological, sociological and historical literature about the socio-economic consequences of neighborhoods. Ironically, however, urban poverty scholars who focus a great deal of attention on the deficits of concentrated poverty neighborhoods have devoted only scant attention to neighborhoods as political units. Even less attention has been devoted to the political relevance of family structure. Although politics is more difficult to recognize when it occurs on street corners and around dining tables than when it occurs in explicitly political institutions, neighborhoods and families are certainly important political units.

According to Matthew Crenson, neighborhoods are most aptly defined as political societies which are animated by agreements among citizens to join together in an effort to ensure safety, comfort, peaceable living and security against those who are not members of society (Crenson 1983). Consequently, neighborhoods derive their political status from the functions that they perform and from the public nature of the neighborhood constituency (Crenson 1983). While many have questioned the viability of neighborhoods as social and political units, the political science literature provides ample evidence of the role that neighborhoods and neighborhood associations have played as political units and effective players in the policy-making process (Easton 1965; Kotler 1969; Morris and Hess 1975; Ostrom 1976).

During the 1960s, for example, neighborhoods were delegated with political authority as conduits for waging the War On Poverty. Operating under the Model Cities and Economic Opportunities Programs, neighborhood associations were the front-line distributors of democracy for urban residents. The federal government in concert with municipal governments delegated some decision-making authority to urban residents through the network of neighborhood associations, which worked effectively to represent and articulate the policy dispositions of neighborhood constituents (Fainstein and Fainstein 1974).

The vitality and effectiveness of neighborhood organizations are also documented in historical accounts of the Machine Politics Era. Just as black churches have served as training grounds for black political leaders, so have neighborhoods functioned as training grounds for political leaders during the Machine Politics Era, and, to an extent also for some contemporary leaders.[2] Moreover, involvement in salient neighborhood and community development issues has often prepared and provided individuals with the tools and civic skills that facilitated subsequent political activity.

Neighborhood associations and neighborhood politics were not only salient during the Machine Politics Era and the 1960s, but they also have the potential of playing a crucial role in contemporary municipal politics. Research has demonstrated the deft and unique ability of some contemporary neighborhood organizations in facilitating direct democracy. More recently, scholars have convincingly demonstrated the usefulness of neighborhood associations as facilitators of direct democracy. According to the research team of Berry, Portney and Thomson, cities which couple strong systems of neighborhood association with direct linkages to municipal policy-making institutions ultimately have higher levels of citizen participation. Such participation has been known to exert a balancing effect on the power equation in cities (Berry, Portney and Thomson 1993). This is especially the case in relations between neighborhood groups and business organizations, which have historically been unbalanced in favor of business interests. As political institutions, neighborhood associations are important in the following ways: (1) citizens articulated the belief that neighborhood associations would offer them the opportunity to become involved in major issues if they wanted to participate; (2) neighborhood associations helped to build a sense of community among urban residents who want to be active in politics; and (3) neighborhood associations were able to empower residents within the existing municipal representational structure (Berry, Portney and Thomson 1993).

What remains to be addressed, however, is the effect of concentrated poverty on the political functions of neighborhoods. After all, if concentrated poverty stifles the economic and social functions of neighborhoods by making them economic wastelands and bastions of social isolation, it is plausible to expect that the concentration of poverty would also impair the political functions of neighborhoods and their residents as viable participants in the municipal decision-making process. Above all, however, the concentration of poverty is expected to impede the neighborhood process of politicization and political stimulation. Beleaguered by poverty and its associated ills, concentrated poverty neighborhoods are expected to be less capable of serving as facilitators of political activity.

Neighborhoods are only one aspect of the complex socio-political milieu of contemporary urban environments. Family context, which is a more proximate source of influence, has received far less attention than neighborhood context, especially as it relates to political behavior. Instead of focusing on political behavior, urban poverty scholars have focused attention on the socio-economic consequences of single-parent households and their implications for educational attainment, socio-economic mobility and inter-generational poverty (McLanahan and Garfinkel 1989). However, there is very little understanding of how single-parent versus two-parent household structures affect political behavior. The socialization literature suggests that families are important political units because they serve as the most proximate sources of influence (Jennings and Niemi 1981; Jennings and Niemi 1974; Jennings and Niemi 1968). Partisan identification, issue preference and electoral behavior are often the function of cues received in the family context (Beck and Jennings 1975; Beck 1976). Subsequent research has also documented the importance of communication between spouses as sources of political information, catalysts and influence on political activity (Huckfeldt and Sprague 1995). While the political consequences of single-parent households have not been addressed by the urban poverty research, there are compelling reasons to expect that individuals in single-parent households may be less involved in the political process.

Furthermore, existing research on urban poverty has done an inadequate job of ferreting out the political consequences of social isolation. Most studies assume that all individuals in single-parent households and concentrated poverty neighborhoods are socially isolated but do not assess or test the empirical efficacy of social isolation as a separate influence. However, research has consistently demonstrated that impoverished inner-city residents have fewer social ties and that they have ties of lesser social values (Wilson and Wacquant 1989; Bordieu 1986; Stack 1974). Also, studies have documented the weak association that some impoverished inner-city residents have with social and religious organizations, and that individuals who live in concentrated poverty neighborhoods are much less likely to belong to organizations than those who reside in low poverty neighborhoods (Wilson and Wacquant 1989; Massey and Denton 1993).

The limited and less valuable social networks as well as the lower levels of organizational membership are relevant for political behavior. Indeed, political participation research has demonstrated the efficacy of social networks in stimulating and facilitating political activity (Huckfeldt and Sprague 1995). Research has also demonstrated that involvement in social and religious organizations provides participants with civic skills and political stimuli that catalyze participation in a host of political activities (Verba, Schlozman and Brady 1995). Therefore, not only is it important to consider the role of concentrated poverty neighborhoods and single-parent households, but it is necessary to understand the political consequences of social isolation as well.

Certainly, scores of studies have demonstrated that participation in the political process matters and that politicians as well as policy-makers are responsive to what they hear (Verba and Nie 1972; Mayhew 1974; Fenno 1978). It is, therefore, important to understand whether or not the reportedly low participation rates among the poor as well as the residents of inner-city communities are affected by debilitating social contexts. Toward that end, this book examines how race, concentrated poverty neighborhoods, social isolation and single-parent households affect the acquisition of politically relevant resources that often lead to political participation as well as the act of participating in electoral and non-electoral political activities. Chapter Two critiques extant theoretical explanations of political participation and develops an alternative model which incorporates the social context of urban communities. It concludes with a chapter-by-chapter overview of the book.

NOTES

1. The political machines provided some ameliorative benefits to urban residents, but they did little to change the structural and institutional impediments of the nineteenth and early-twentieth-century cities (Erie 1988).

2. Two of the mayors of Columbus, Ohio, emerged from the Hilltop neighborhood, which is well known in Columbus for its political activism. Chapter Three provides a more detailed account of this neighborhood and its role in the study.

CHAPTER 2

Toward a Theory of Urban Political Behavior

Political scientists have relied on three major theoretical frameworks to explain participation among individual American citizens. These theories underscore the importance of either socio-economic status (SES), cost-benefit analysis or contextual factors in explaining political participation. However, none of them addresses the unique social context in which inner-city residents are embedded. The goal of this chapter is to provide a critique of the three models and to delineate the alternative model of political participation that will be utilized in this study.

THE SES MODEL OF POLITICAL PARTICIPATION

The standard SES model of political participation is predicated on the assertion that socio-economic status plays a pre-eminent role in predicting the political orientations and behaviors of individuals (Verba and Nie 1972; Campbell, Converse, Miller and Stokes 1960; Wolfinger and Rosenstone 1980). Studies have invariably demonstrated the empirical power of this model, as individuals with higher levels of income, education and occupational prestige are more likely to be politically active than their counterparts who possess lower levels of the foregoing attributes. Subsequent studies have disaggregated the SES variable to show how occupation, income and especially education differentially influence voting activity (Wolfinger and Rosenstone 1980).

While vitally important in explaining political participation, the SES model is found lacking for its inability to specify the mechanisms through which the influences of SES affect political participation (Brady, Verba and Schlozman 1995). For example, while the SES model is able to predict that the poor will participate less frequently than their middle-class counterparts, it is incapable of specifying how lower levels of education, income and occupational prestige limit participation in a variety of political activities.

A recent revision of the SES model of political participation has made progress in explaining the mechanisms of SES influence on political participation. Dubbed the Civic Volunteerism Model (Verba, Schlozman and Brady 1995), it improves on the SES model by emphasizing the importance of resources like time, money and civic skills. It has also addressed a serious theoretical flaw in the SES model by illustrating how these unequally distributed resources serve as mechanisms for the influence of socio-economic status (SES) on various forms of political participation (Brady, Verba and Schlozman 1995; Verba, Schlozman, Brady and Nie 1993; Schlozman, Burns and Verba 1994). Moreover, the resource-centered explanation demonstrates how the lack of civic resources explains gender as well as racial-cum-ethnic differences in political participation (Verba, Schlozman, Brady and Nie 1993; Schlozman, Burns, Verba and Donahue 1995).

RATIONAL-CHOICE THEORY

While the traditional SES model of political participation is rich in empirical precision, the rational-choice theory of political participation is rich in theory. Based on cost-benefit economic analysis, rational-choice theory attempts to explain the benefits of participating in politics and the extent to which those benefits justify the costs of participation. According to rational-choice theorists, citizens are rational actors who invariably try to maximize participatory outcomes. For example, sometimes it is more rational to benefit from the participation activities of others than to exact costs for participating when the return may be small. Contrary to the postulates of earlier versions of rational-choice theory, a substantial proportion of the American population participates in electoral activities. Scholars explain the lack of empirical congruence in terms of psychological benefits (Riker and Ordeshook 1968) and group-based effectiveness (Opp 1986). Other researchers have argued that rational choice theory is empirically bankrupt because of faulty theoretical assumptions (Aldrich 1993; Mansbridge 1990). Still others have agreed that the validity of rational-choice theory rests on how the term "rational" is defined (Conway 1991).

CONTEXTUAL THEORIES OF POLITICAL PARTICIPATION

While rational-choice theory and the SES models of political participation focus on individual-level factors in explaining political participation, contextual theories of political behavior are based on the proposition that individuals are rooted in inter-dependent contexts that ultimately influence political participation. Such theories have posited that political attitudes and behaviors are the products of individual preferences as well as the preferences of individuals in relevant neighborhood and family contexts (Huckfeldt, Plutzer and Sprague 1993; Huckfeldt and Sprague 1991; Huckfeldt and Sprague 1987; Knoke 1990).

While political participation studies have documented the direct effects of contextual influences with specific emphasis on four factors, namely family context (Jennings and Niemi 1968, 1974, 1981); neighborhood context (Huckfeldt 1986, 1979, 1983; Giles, Wright and Dantico 1981; Huckfeldt and Sprague 1988; Crenson 1983); the occupational context (Finifter 1974) and the religious context (Wald 1987; Wald, Owen and Hill 1988; Harris 1994), most contextual analyses have focused on neighborhood influences. Initial studies showed how white racial attitudes and voting behavior varied according to the concentration of black populations (Key 1949; Prothro 1963; Wright 1976, 1977; Bobo and Gilliam 1990; Huckfeldt and Kohfeld 1989; Walton 1985; Carmines and Stimson 1989; Giles 1977; Giles and Hertz 1994; Giles and Buckner 1993). Subsequent research focused on the extent to which neighborhood context has important political consequences as it influences partisan identification, satisfaction with neighborhood municipal services, political participation and friendship networks (Huckfeldt 1986; Giles, Wright and Dantico 1981; Langston and Rapoport 1975; Segal and Meyer 1969; Walton 1985).

Contextual research has also shown that socially based activities like campaigning and petitioning as opposed to individual actions like voting are more likely to be affected by neighborhood status (Huckfeldt 1986). Also, other studies have demonstrated that neighborhood context is more important in explaining political participation than political orientations (Giles, Wright and Dantico 1981) and still other studies have demonstrated the importance of context for public policy-making (Carmines and Stimson 1989).

Contextual theories of political participation also specify that various forms of voluntary and involuntary social interactions serve as mechanisms through which contextual effects influence political participation (Huckfeldt and Sprague 1995; McPhee 1963; Huckfeldt 1986; MacKuen and Brown 1987). Specifically, such studies have demonstrated that social interaction and social networks serve as mechanisms for the influence of contextual effects on political behavior (Huckfeldt and Sprague 1987; Huckfeldt 1983; Huckfeldt and Sprague 1988; Huckfeldt and Sprague 1995).

CRITIQUE OF SES, RATIONAL-CHOICE AND CONTEXTUAL MODELS OF POLITICAL PARTICIPATION

In many respects, the aforementioned theories have gone a long way to further our understanding of political participation. However, they do not incorporate variables that are crucial in explaining the political activities of inner-city residents. For example, most of the existing political participation studies have focused on explaining electoral as opposed to non-electoral participation, although the latter has historically been important for impoverished and other disfranchised groups (Morris 1984). African Americans and women were disfranchised from the political system and unable to utilize the vote to ventilate political grievances. As a result, members of these minority groups staged protests, contacted political officials and organized petition drives in an effort to catapult their issues to the fore-front of the policy-making agenda.

Political participation theories and research have also largely been geared toward the activities of whites, with relatively little focus on minority aspects of political participation (Walton 1985; Walton 1994); and a majority of the political participation research is based on large national election studies with little emphasis on inner-city or other local contexts. As Chapter One demonstrated, the socio-political context of inner-city communities across the United States has changed tremendously over the last two decades. These transformations demand more inclusive models of political participation which integrate the unique experiences and social contexts of inner-city Americans. Such studies also necessitate a contextual approach to data collection, whereby individuals can be analyzed within specific social contexts.

FOCUS ON INDIVIDUAL-LEVEL FACTORS

While the standard SES, rational-choice and civic volunteerism models of political participation differ in the concepts utilized to explain political participation, all of them focus primarily on individual characteristics to the exclusion of contextual factors in explaining political orientations and behavior.

As a consequence of focusing an inordinate amount of attention on the relationship existing among socio-economic status, political orientations and political behavior without considering contextual variations, participation scholars erroneously assume that individuals having the same socio-economic status, respond similarly toward the political system despite differences in their neighborhood and family contexts (Kuo 1977). At the same time, such scholars fail to address the more interesting question of the extent to which contextual variations exert a differentiating influence on the political orientations and behavior of individuals. Indeed, several queries come into play here: For example, is it plausible to assume that poor individuals in working class and concentrated poverty neighborhoods, respectively, have equal access to economic and politically relevant resources? Or, do adults who head single-parent households have as much unfettered access to economic and politically relevant resources as adults who are embedded in two-parent households? Moreover, is it plausible to assume that poor individuals in working-class and concentrated poverty neighborhoods participate in politics at the same levels? Unfortunately, these are questions that remain largely unaddressed in the political participation literature.

CONTEXT, CLASS AND RACE

While contextual theories of political participation address the lack of emphasis on context in explaining the political participation of individual citizens, they often focus on a single environment like neighborhood context or religious context, without exploring the multi-faceted contexts in which individuals are embedded (Huckfeldt, Plutzer and Sprague 1993). This flaw is unfortunate as American political behavior is influenced by a host of interactions in various religious, family, occupational and neighborhood contexts. It is especially tragic as research has shown that many inner-city residents face a multitude of barriers at the family and neighborhood levels. Empirical assessments of poor individuals in a variety of contexts would greatly supplement our knowledge about how poverty at both the individual and contextual levels influences political participation.

Contextual theories of political participation are also limited by their focus on middle- and working-class neighborhoods predominated by whites. Only recently have studies focused on the effects of living in concentrated poverty neighborhoods, and the two sets of findings present a conflicting picture of the importance of neighborhood context. One study examined the influence of neighborhood context on poor whites and blacks. Contrary to expectations, the findings demonstrated that there was no significant political participation nor any attitudinal differences among poor people who live in poor and nonpoor neighborhoods (Berry, Portney and Thomson 1991). A second study focused specifically on African Americans and reported significant racial differences in participation and attitudes of African Americans in concentrated poverty neighborhoods and those living in working and middle-class neighborhoods (Cohen and Dawson 1993). Additional research and a broader theoretical framework are needed to reconcile these differences.

POLITICAL PARTICIPATION: THE OVER-EMPHASIS ON ELECTORAL ACTIVITY

Theories of political participation are limited by a focus on electoral participation, especially voting. However, if voting is the hallmark of democracy in America, then American democracy indeed, has a lot of limitations. After all, voting is an individual activity which occurs infrequently as compared with other forms of political activity, and an increasing proportion of the population fails to vote every year. However, citizens are capable of participating in politics by involving themselves in a host of non-electoral activities, from contacting political officials to working together to solve community problems to participating in demonstrations and protest marches. Since non-electoral activities like demonstrating, protesting, and contacting public officials were employed by disfranchised and disenfranchised groups before they were capable of utilizing the ballot box, it is essential to have a theory of political participation which includes both electoral as well as non-electoral activities. Empirically examining various forms of political participation is a necessity if a more general theory of political participation is to be developed (Conway 1991).

ALTERNATIVE MODEL OF POLITICAL PARTICIPATION

The alternative model of political participation that will be utilized in this study differs from previous explanations of political behavior in its attempt to explain political participation among inner-city residents. The model is undergirded by the proposition that residents are embedded in a series of important contexts, which structure social interaction and are consequential for political behavior. These social contexts are expected to directly influence both electoral and non-electoral participation. However, a unique aspect of this study is its attempt to assess the indirect influences of inner-city social contexts on political behavior. In this respect, two factors are important. First, it is hypothesized that concentrated poverty neighborhoods and single-parent households facilitate social isolation, which limits interaction with "upwardly mobile" individuals who are connected to mainstream social, economic and political institutions. As induced by the debilitating social contexts, social isolation is expected to depress involvement in both electoral and non-electoral activities.

The second factor that is expected to serve as a conduit for contextual influences on political participation is socio-political resources. Similar to economic and social resources, socio-political resources are skills, associations and psychological attachments that facilitate and catalyze political participation. Concentrated poverty neighborhoods and single-parent households are expected to limit access to socio-political resources and thereby depress involvement in electoral and non-electoral activities.

The alternative model of political participation that will be utilized for this study is based on the proposition that political participation is an important mechanism through which citizen preferences and public opinion are relayed to policy-makers. In contrast to the over-emphasis on electoral participation, the alternative model of political participation includes a wide array of non-electoral activities, including attending community meetings, contracting political officials, attending protest marches as well as demonstrations, signing petitions in support of candidates or issues, and working together to solve community problems.

Race is also expected to play a significant role in the political behavior of inner-city residents. Specifically, blacks are expected to be more disadvantaged than their white counterparts in terms of socio-political resources because blacks have endured the problems of concentrated poverty neighborhoods and social isolation more often and for longer periods of time. Consequently, compared to whites, the political behavior of blacks is expected to be more susceptible to the detrimental influences of concentrated poverty neighborhoods, single-parent households and social isolation.

Figure 2.1 illustrates the model that is to be explored in this study. Consistent with the foregoing expectations, it includes both endogenous (neighborhood context, family context, income, education and gender) as well as exogenous factors (social isolation, socio-political resources and political participation). The components of the model are discussed below.

THE SOCIAL CONTEXT OF POLITICAL PARTICIPATION

Neighborhood Context

Most research on the political consequences of social contexts have focused on neighborhood context with an emphasis on middle and working class communities. Only recently have studies focused on the growing problem of poor and concentrated poverty neighborhoods in American cities (Cohen and Dawson 1993; Berry, Portney and Thomson 1991). Studies have shown that in comparison to neighborhoods with lower percentages of poverty, concentrated poverty neighborhoods are characterized as having limited employment opportunities, a lack of social networks, higher incidents of crime, a dearth of conventional and law-abiding role models and lower levels of politically involved citizens (Wilson 1987; Sampson 1987; Kasarda 1989; Sullivan 1989; Cohen and Dawson 1993). The alarming rates of criminal activity coupled with the geographic isolation of concentrated poverty neighborhoods and the lack of viable institutions in such communities is expected to depress the electoral participation of residents. In keeping with previous studies on white working-class and middle-class neighborhoods, the non-electoral activity of inner-city residents is expected to be more profoundly impacted by neighborhood context, since it often involves social interaction and the collective activity of neighborhood residents (Huckfeldt 1986).

Figure 2.1
Theoretical Model

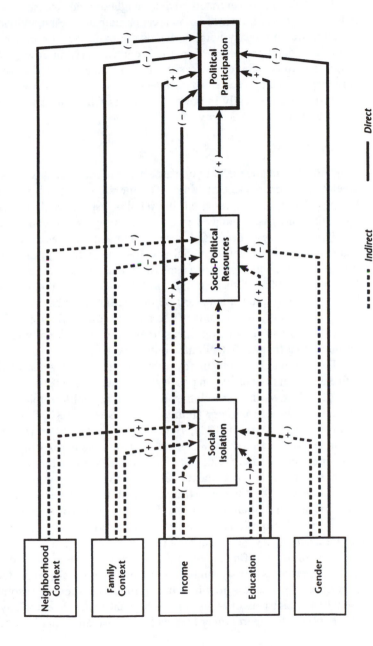

Residence in concentrated poverty neighborhoods is also expected to have an indirect influence on political participation. First, individuals in concentrated poverty neighborhoods are expected to report higher levels of social isolation than their counterparts in low poverty neighborhoods. Second, residents of concentrated poverty neighborhoods are expected to have less access to social networks and organizations, politically important resources which are known to be facilitators of political activity.

Family Context

Neighborhood context is only one aspect of the social context in which inner-city residents are embedded. The literature on family structure has postulated that single-parent households, especially those headed by women, are disadvantaged in a number of areas, including greater psychological stress, decreased income, frequent changes in residence and employment as well as social isolation in the form of diminished social networks and support systems (McLanahan and Garfinkel 1989; McLanahan 1995). Other studies have suggested that mother-only households have played a major role in creating the urban underclass. Also, mother-only households are less likely to benefit from durable ties to social and religious organizations or other politically relevant resources that frequently facilitate political participation.

Political participation studies have only infrequently analyzed the influence of family context on political orientations and behavior, and a majority of the recent research has focused on the political relevance of marital discussion partners (Jennings and Niemi 1981; Stoker and Jennings 1995; Marsden 1987; Beck 1991; Straits 1991). The extant urban poverty research also documents its relevance for explanations of urban political behavior. Characterized as either two-parent or single-parent structures, family context is expected to have important political consequences. The time constraints and limited resources that are endemic to single-parent households are expected to diminish the opportunity for participation in political activities, especially non-electoral activities which require more time and collective efforts.

The indirect influence of family context is expected in two different respects. First, single-parent households are expected to experience less access to important politically relevant resources, including social networks and organizational involvement. They are also expected to report higher levels of social isolation and have fewer social ties with other families and individuals, which, in turn, limit the possibility of social and political interaction.

SOCIAL ISOLATION

Social isolation has been identified as the mechanism through which the effects of neighborhood context and family context influence the social and economic behaviors of inner-city residents (Wilson 1987, Wilson and Wacquant 1989). The concept is utilized most frequently in structural theories of urban poverty as an alternative to the culture of poverty. Such explanations emphasize the lack of involvement with institutions and individuals who represent mainstream society. In concert with these theories, it is hypothesized that social isolation diminishes access to resources which facilitate political participation. Moreover, isolation from mainstream institutions and individuals that have traditionally reinforced the importance of participation in the electoral process are undoubtedly expected to diminish participation, especially in voting activities. This is especially so since a great deal of social communication influences the political behavior of individuals (Huckfeldt and Sprague 1995). Such studies have demonstrated that political discussion during an election campaign is an important mechanism of social influence which is intricately tied to social contexts (Huckfeldt and Sprague 1991). Other studies have demonstrated that individuals are differentially influenced by political communication as a function of contextual factors and patterns of interaction (Huckfeldt and Sprague 1995).

SOCIO-POLITICAL RESOURCES

Recent political behavior research has emphasized the importance of resources as facilitators of political participation. Organizational affiliation, civic skills, psychological engagement in politics and religious involvement all go a long way to increase the likelihood that individuals will actively participate in the political arena. Psychological engagement measures individuals' attachment to politics as evinced by a variety of attitudes, beliefs and values (Abramson 1983; Brody 1978; Conway 1991). The higher the level of psychological engagement, the greater the level of participation. Additionally, the traditional components of psychological engagement are internal and external political efficacy, interest in political affairs, strength of partisan identification and civic virtue.

Other important socio-political resources include involvement in social and religious organizations. Such institutional affiliation equips individuals with a host of politically relevant skills like letter writing, contacting political officials and organizing events which, in turn, catalyze political participation. Also, such organizations frequently serve as sites for political discussions which also elevate interest in politics and catalyze participation. It is important therefore, to assess how debilitating social contexts affect access to socio-political resources, which play a crucial role in facilitating participation in both electoral and non-electoral activities.

CONTROL VARIABLES

Studies of political participation have invariably demonstrated that in both electoral and non-electoral activities, participants are disproportionately wealthy, well educated, male and white. It is important, therefore, for a study which emphasizes the importance of contextual factors to control for the influences of income and education as well as gender and race in an effort to understand the viability of contextual factors.

Income

The relationship between income and political participation is well documented in the political behavior literature (Wolfinger and Rosenstone 1980; Milbrath 1965; Lane 1959; Lipset 1960; Conway 1991). The more money individuals have, the more likely they are to participate in political activities. Such findings are understandable as individuals with money can afford to do more than their counterparts who do not have discretionary income. For example, they can contribute to political campaigns and issues. Money can also be utilized to purchase other resources that make it easier to participate in politics including time and automobiles. Additionally, the poor spend so much time trying to make ends meet that there is little remaining time for the luxury of political participation.

Education

Among the socio-economic status predictors of political participation, income plays the most important role in influencing political participation. The salutary effects of education are not only evident with electoral activities but non-electoral activities as well. Education imparts skills that are relevant to political participation. It places individuals in important institutional settings and fosters interest in politics—all of which are very important ingredients of political participation (Verba, Schlozman and Brady 1995). The direct influences of education on political participation are also important. Education allows individuals to surmount the barriers to participation (Wolfinger and Rosenstone 1980). Individuals with higher levels of education are more likely to follow political events and harbor strong opinions about issues—two factors which facilitate political activity.

Gender

Urban poverty and political participation research have documented the importance of gender in explaining various behaviors. Past research on the urban underclass has shown that men are particularly sensitive to problems of joblessness, while women are often associated with the inter-generational transmission of poverty and social isolation (Wilson 1987, 1996). Meanwhile, the electoral behavior research has demonstrated that the erstwhile voting turnout gap between men and women is nonexistent, especially when age and education are held constant (Baxter and Lansing 1983). However, differences are evident between men and women in non-electoral activities and in attitudes and beliefs associated with political participation, thus making it important to control for the effects of gender.

Race

Contextual factors have always played a crucial role in explanations of black political behavior (Walton 1985, 1994). Racial composition, political mobilization, policy context and voting registration as well as electoral laws go a long way to explain the racial disparities in voting before the 1960s, whereby blacks were much less likely than their white counterparts to vote in local and national elections. Since the enactment of voting rights legislation and the enforcement of voting rights laws, the gap between whites and blacks has narrowed considerably. However, contemporary studies have varied in their assessment of the white-black voting gap. Existing research on the relationship between political participation and race demonstrates that blacks vote less than whites. Other studies, however, have cautioned against using voting as a measure of political participation because racial differences vary across modes of political participation (Verba and Nie 1972). Still, other studies have demonstrated that racial differences are significantly minimized and sometimes favor minorities when SES controls are utilized (Olsen 1970; Orum 1966; Gutterbock and London 1983; Verba and Nie 1972).

This study will examine racial differences in the political behavior of white and black inner-city residents as a function of social context. Toward that end, separate bivariate analyses and path models will be computed for whites and blacks. Furthermore, statistical tests for racial differences will be computed for the path models in an effort to discern whether or not the coefficients for whites and blacks are statistically distinguishable.

OVERVIEW OF THE STUDY

A valid empirical assessment of the model (Figure 2.1) is contingent upon the availability of appropriate data and the articulation of lucid and theoretically plausible hypotheses. The data set that will be utilized to empirically assess the alternative model of political participation is described in Chapter Three. The chapter also provides a rationale for the neighborhood and municipal setting of the study, as well as a discussion of the questionnaire and design methodology.

The book is organized around five hypotheses and they will be evaluated in two separate stages. The first stage assesses bivariate relationships between a single aspect of the inner-city social context and political behavior. The second stage utilizes multivariate causal analysis to simultaneously assess various aspects of inner-city social contexts on political behavior.

Chapter Four assesses the extent to which racial differentiation exists in the social and political behavior of white and black residents in concentrated poverty neighborhoods. The hypothesis undergirding the analysis in Chapter Four posits that the social context of the community will play a larger role in determining the behavior of individuals than race. The findings are relevant in the sense that policy-makers have defined the problems of inner-city American communities as "black" or "minority" problems. However, if whites and blacks in similar social contexts behave similarly despite racial differences, then policy-makers are compelled to examine the contextual forces that dictate behavior instead of focusing merely on racial factors.

Examined in Chapter Five is the extent to which whites and blacks in concentrated poverty communities experience social isolation as well as a disconnection from social and religious institutions above and beyond the influence of individual income. The hypothesis flowing from this study is that social isolation—the lack of interaction with individuals and institutions who represent mainstream society—facilitates economic marginalization, diminishes access to political participation and erodes participation in politics. Since social isolation is deemed as a mechanism for the debilitating influences of social contexts, it is important to understand the extent to which individuals in concentrated poverty communities exhibit signs of social isolation.

Chapter Six examines the hypothesis that residence in concentrated poverty neighborhoods diminishes participation in electoral and non-electoral activities and fosters negative political orientations, while Chapter Seven assesses the extent to which individuals in single-parent households will experience more economic marginalization, participate less in political activities and harbor more negative orientations toward the political system.

Chapter Eight assesses the direct and indirect influences of various social contexts on political behavior. It also provides a statistical test of racial differences. Chapter Nine summarizes the findings and delineates their relevance for the broader urban poverty and political participation literatures.

CHAPTER 3

The Site of the Study

INTRODUCTION

Several aspects of the analyses of urban political behavior are not only stymied by inappropriate theoretical frameworks, but by a lack of suitable data. The model of political participation, utilized in this study posits that individual political activity occurs within a set of specific social contexts. This theoretical framework necessitates both individual- and contextual-level data. Consequently, the purpose of Chapter Three is to describe the data set that will be utilized in the study, its neighborhood and municipal settings as well as the rationale for survey design and methodology.

Historically, the lack of adequate contextual-cum-individual-level data has prevented past researchers from fully understanding how various urban contexts influence political behavior. For example, the large American National Election Studies rarely over-sample among the poor, and do not include enough neighborhood and census tract information to facilitate contextual analyses. While the Detroit Area Study for 1989, for example, collects data in poor areas, it largely focuses on policy and sociological issues and does not have many direct measures of participation. As a result, scholars interested in studying the political behavior of inner-city residents and the poor have to conduct specialized surveys to gather the needed information.

This study, however, utilizes a unique data set, which includes contextual- as well as individual-level data to examine the direct and indirect influence of the current inner-city social milieu, which has included spatially isolated, concentrated poverty neighborhoods, single-parent households, and social isolation on the political participation of inner-city residents. As it is typical of many urban and contextual analyses, this research has succeeded in focusing on a particular community, the Ohio state capital of Columbus. Interestingly, the city is an ideal case-study context for various reasons, including the following: that, first, it is a frostbelt city, which has experienced massive job loss in the manufacturing sector that once served as the economic backbone for city residents by providing good jobs for poorly skilled and under-educated workers. Second, in part as a consequence of de-industrialization, Columbus was one of the ten cities that witnessed the largest increase in the number of ghetto poor between 1970 and 1980 (Jargowsky and Bane 1991). Third, the ghetto-poor population in Columbus is not only made up of blacks, but also has a significant number of whites.

THE EMERGENCE OF NEIGHBORHOOD POLITICS

The city of Columbus is noted for its efforts to involve citizens in local government decision making. Prior to 1983, civic organizations were the major organizational vehicles that citizens utilized to influence local policy-making. In the early 1980s, however, the mayor of Columbus realized that it was virtually impossible to respond to the needs and concerns of over 300 civic organizations. Consequently, he established area commissions, which became mandated in the Columbus city charter and were used to reorganize the manner in which citizens of Columbus expressed their concerns to the mayor and the city council. Instead of responding to disparate civic organizations, citizens were given the organizational mechanism to effect policy changes through neighborhood organizations.

While neighborhood area commissions are mandated in the Columbus City Charter, residents in specific areas of the city had to accomplish a number of organizational tasks before their respective area commission was approved. Additionally, while neighborhood residents are endowed with the responsibility of selecting their own leaders or commissioners, all elected representative choices are subject to mayoral approval. Thus, Columbus serves as a site which includes social contexts of concentrated poverty neighborhoods predominated by whites as well as blacks and an optimal political environment, which encourages citizen involvement in neighborhood associations.

NEIGHBORHOOD SELECTION

The data for the analysis come from four different neighborhood contexts in Columbus, namely Franklinton, a predominantly white, concentrated poverty neighborhood; South Linden, a predominantly black, concentrated poverty neighborhood; Hilltop, a predominantly white low poverty neighborhood and North Central, a predominantly black low poverty neighborhood. All of the four neighborhoods have active area commissions, although the commissions vary in age and nature of activity.

As Table 3.1 demonstrates, there are gross disparities across concentrated poverty and low poverty tracts in the city of Columbus in terms of poverty level, educational attainment, and labor force participation. Compared with 12% of citywide residents who live below the poverty line, the poverty rates are alarming in the concentrated poverty neighborhoods of Franklinton and South Linden, where almost half of all neighborhood residents live below the poverty line. The poverty rates in the low poverty neighborhoods of Hilltop and North Central are much lower (20%) than those in concentrated poverty neighborhoods, but they are still considerably higher than the citywide average.

Table 3.1

Neighborhood and Citywide Statistics

Indicators	Citywide	Franklinton	Hilltop	South Linden	North Central
People below poverty	12%	49%	20%	49%	21%
People without high school degree	19	52	37	49	37
Percent black	23	16	4	91	90

Additionally, while over 80% of Columbus residents citywide have earned high school diplomas or above, only about 50% of residents in the concentrated poverty neighborhoods reported having a high school diploma. The disparities are even more alarming among residents with bachelor's degrees and above. Less than 5% of residents in concentrated poverty neighborhoods reported possessing a college degree, compared with almost 30% of the at-large Columbus residents. Table 3.1 also provides some statistics on labor force participation.

Unemployment among Columbus residents is relatively low. However, the unemployment rates among residents in concentrated poverty neighborhoods reveals that, compared with residents in low poverty neighborhoods, such residents have serious problems obtaining and keeping jobs that are commensurate with their skills. Finally, the statistics also illustrate the level of racial segregation in Columbus, whereby whites and blacks, respectively, live in neighborhoods predominated by other whites and blacks. The data also reveal that Columbus is a city that is predominated by whites, as blacks comprise less than 30% of the population.

In this study, census tracts were utilized as proxies for neighborhood context.[1] However, in the case of neighborhoods selected for this study, census boundaries generally conform with neighborhood boundaries set by the city of Columbus. Therefore, residents in each of the four neighborhoods were not merely assigned to a neighborhood context; rather, their political orientations and behaviors were examined in light of perceived neighborhood boundaries.

The neighborhood-cum-census tracts were selected on the basis of three criteria. First, neighborhoods were selected as a result of poverty rates, whereby concentrated poverty neighborhoods were characterized by poverty rates of 40%, while low poverty neighborhoods were characterized by poverty rates of 20%. While there is adequate variation between the two neighborhood contexts, it is crucial to understand and appreciate that this is a very strict test of structural theories of urban poverty in general and Wilson's notion of concentrated poverty neighborhoods in particular. The analysis does not examine middle-class versus concentrated poverty neighborhoods. Instead, it examines the differences at varying levels of poverty whereby a new kind of urban poverty is differentiated from neighborhoods commonly known as ghettos or poor. To the extent that differences are found among individuals in concentrated poverty and low poverty neighborhoods, much larger differences are expected when middle-class neighborhoods are compared with concentrated poverty neighborhoods. The next section of the chapter provides a descriptive overview of the neighborhoods selected for the study. They include the concentrated poverty neighborhoods of Franklinton and South Linden and the low poverty neighborhoods of Hilltop and North Central.

FRANKLINTON

> We have a lot of people who are interested in making things better. There is high interest in neighborhood issues, but it depends on where your interest lies. Some people don't see the commission as a way to get involved. For them, it's just politics.[2]

Two high poverty neighborhoods were selected for the study, including the predominantly white neighborhood of Franklinton and the predominantly black neighborhood of South Linden. Known as the original site of the city of Columbus, the community of Franklinton was founded in 1797 by Lucus Sullivant, a surveyor for the United States government (Ware 1991). The first development occurred on Gift Street, which is the oldest street in the city.[3] The mid-nineteenth century ushered in growth to the Franklinton community as the Industrial Revolution spurred the production of railroad cars and horse-drawn carriages (Ware 1991). People from surrounding towns moved to Franklinton to take advantage of this industrial activity (Ware 1991).

Growth and prosperity were not to be Franklinton's legacy, however, as the flood of 1913 destroyed homes and businesses, claimed lives and eventually drove many of Franklinton's prosperous families and thriving businesses to higher grounds on the Hilltop and other areas of the city (Ware 1991). Homes in Franklinton lost as much as 50% of their value, and Franklinton's growth was also impeded by the post-war suburbanization boom. Stable families and businesses moved to more placid suburban environments and their exodus was followed by a migration of low-income families. Dubbed the "Bottoms" because of its floodplain location, Franklinton is also home to a large population of poor Appalachians. Although it is also home to some manufacturing sites, social service is the most prominent community industry, as the income of Franklinton residents comprises only half of the Franklin County average. Approximately 35% of the residents are children and two-thirds of all these children drop out of school before graduation (Ware 1991). Franklinton also houses several types of parks and recreation centers, including Dodge Park and McKinley Park, along with a host of other informal gathering places that are scattered along some of the residential streets.

Franklinton is located within walking distance of downtown, but the inner-belt construction forms a barrier that physically isolates Franklinton from the other parts of the city. It is surrounded by highways, railroads and rivers. In accordance with a city code enacted in 1983, development was restricted in the floodplain, which comprises a large portion of Franklinton. The code brought development in Franklinton to a virtual standstill as it restricted new construction and renovation of existing structures in excess of 50% of the current value. Exceptions were granted only if the buildings were flood proof, a prohibitively expensive undertaking. Consequently, efforts to substantially rehabilitate and construct new housing in the area were virtually non-existent. Also problematic is the high number of rental housing units, including low-income housing projects that are indicative of diminished neighborhood stability and cohesiveness, property neglect and disrepair.

However, as indicated by the foregoing opening quotation, in a July 1997 interview given by Helen Evans of the Franklinton Area Commission, neighborhood leaders have not lost hope in their area or in the ability of residents to make positive contributions. In a large measure, they have waged a successful organizational battle to resuscitate Franklinton. A most important aspect of this battle is the construction of a floodwall, which will revitalize business in the community. In an effort to make the floodwall a reality, members of the Franklinton Area Neighborhood Commission sought and received the assistance of the Franklinton business community (which is known as the Franklinton Board of Trade), state representatives, the Corps of Engineers, and U.S. congressmen Glenn and Wiley. With the determination of neighborhood residents and the help of important political officials, Franklinton has witnessed the construction of the levee, which is the first important step in the construction of a floodwall. In commenting on this successful achievement, Ms. Evans further made the following statement: "The most important aspect of our neighborhood activities is the networking piece. We all want our neighborhood to be better. The commission doesn't do anything on its own. That is the way to succeed; in making your neighborhood a better place is to work with others, including politicians, libraries, churches, social service agencies and other neighborhood organizations."

Networking has also been important as Franklinton officials try to tackle neighborhood housing problems. Residents have worked with the Columbus Neighborhood Housing Service to purchase as well as rebuild homes and sell them to individuals at no profit. In fact, the Commission has established a committee to work with the city's health department in trying to clean up run-down housing.

With all of the hard work and efforts, however, Ms. Evans noted that Franklinton, like other low-income neighborhoods, has its share of societal problems, including crime, vandalism, drugs and substandard housing, which is a haven for crime. She stated that one of the important ways to change things in the neighborhood is also through voting. Her comments on the voting participation of neighborhood residents, however, revealed that residents are more involved in neighborhood activities than with the formal process of voting. She explained that "people don't vote as much as they get involved in neighborhood issues. I don't know why. We have been trying to get them to vote, but I think it is because they are frustrated. They want everything to happen now. Even, when there is controversy with other people in the neighborhood, residents often forget that the people who are causing trouble also have rights. People get frustrated because government doesn't work fast enough for them. They then figure, why should I vote?"

In the final analysis, however, Ms. Evans said "I have to commend the city in making citizen involvement possible because the duty of the commission is to make the city aware of neighborhood problems."

SOUTH LINDEN

We do not, we do not have the professional, influential persons with clout living within our neighborhood, who can pick up the telephone and call the mayor and say fix this pothole in front of my house. Until the black community recognizes that it does have the clout, it does not need the money but it does have the clout: the clout is the vote and until we recognize the power of that vote, then, we will have to go downtown and lobby city council for services that they automatically provide for other neighborhoods. . . . We have to learn to use the system that works against us to work for us. The universities are not teaching that, and I don't have an audience to teach it to.[4]

They (black professionals and middle class) take the dollars and the needed training with them. They move out, but they never come back to help.[5]

The quotations above represent the views of Clarence Lumpkin, a founding member of the South Linden Area Commission. His words characterize the problems of inadequate city services, racial-cum-political inexperience and the exodus of the black middle class from inner-city communities that are utilized in many studies of contemporary urban poverty neighborhoods. It is also important to note that his lamentations about the lack of access to political officials are in direct contrast to the experiences of Helen Evans, who is a member of the predominantly white Franklinton Area Commission.

The historical roots of South Linden date back to 1800, when President John Adams granted 4,000 acres of land to George Stevenson in what is presently known as the Linden Area (Urban Land Institute 1992). South Linden, the area that is explored in this study, was established as Linden Heights in 1893 (Urban Land Institute 1992). During the early and mid-twentieth century, Linden Heights was considered to be the most prestigious suburban area north of the city of Columbus. It continued to grow and was finally annexed by the city in 1921 (Urban Land Institute 1992). With the advent of suburbanization and white flight, the construction of new highways and suburban shops, South Linden slid into decline. Poorer residents, who were displaced by highway construction and urban renewal projects, took up residence in the area (Urban Land Institute 1992).

South Linden is, primarily, a residential area with a few commercial and industrial sites scattered throughout some neighborhoods. Its housing stock consists mostly of 1950s-style ranch and Cape Cod construction (Urban Land Institute 1992). Housing conditions generally range from average to good because the area residents have benefitted from revitalization money. However, the housing condition can vary substantially from block to block. About 80% of the homes in South Linden are single-family dwellings, while over 50% of the homes are owner occupied (Urban Land Institute 1992). Almost 20% of the homes are subsidized, and the southeast portion of the neighborhood includes a large public housing project known as Windsor Terrace (Urban Land Institute 1992).

South Linden is also the home of about 30 churches, a large housing project and social service agencies. However, it lacks recreational facilities and play areas for children and only one park is found within its boundaries. According to Mr. Lumpkin, churches have abandoned their social mission in the communities. They rarely perform any outreach activities or teach about social morality. This lack of training, which historically occurred in Sunday schools and morning church worship sessions, has removed the social stigma of pre-marital sex, abortion and out-of-wedlock births. While such behaviors were censured in the black church of the 1960s and 1970s, Lumpkin and other community leaders argue that these problematic social behaviors are now taken as being normal and commonplace.

Like the Franklinton commission, South Linden is also involved in efforts to improve the conditions of life for area residents. Toward that end, they have staged a number of marches and demonstrations to decry and bring attention to the scourge of crack and chemical dependency in the community. They have also worked with a number of community organizations, including the Downtown Columbus Incorporated (DCI) and Private Industrial Council (PIC). These organizations have provided job training opportunities for drop-outs and unwed mothers in the community as well as money for economic development. According to Mr. Lumpkin, the commission has also been active in protesting zoning ordinance laws, which would be detrimental to the community, and they have worked invariably on clean-up and beautification projects.

In its more glorious days, Cleveland Avenue was the major shopping corridor in South Linden.[6] However, the construction of the freeways and the Northern Lights Shopping Center drew customers away and shops along the avenue soon closed. South Linden currently has no commercial core or significant concentration of commercial spaces. Instead, it is disproportionately occupied by check-cashing operations, and immigrant-owned grocery shops.

Unlike Franklinton, however, the prospects for future development are bleak. On-street parking is currently restricted on Cleveland Avenue, which undermines the viability of businesses and economic activity. Additionally, South Linden is plagued by a number of problems, including the high levels of poverty, unemployment and crime, poor land use, and the large number of children in its population. Above all, however, is the detrimental impact that the deteriorating Cleveland Avenue and erstwhile shopping corridor have on the appearance, viability and reputation of the South Linden community.

Also, unlike leaders in Franklinton, who expressed optimistic views about the direction of their community, some community leaders in South Linden are seemingly overwhelmed by the intransigence of neighborhood problems. They argue that race plays an important factor in community development decisions, and that the main artery is seen as a viable route for suburban traffic but not economic development. Moreover, some commissioners have cited the transient nature of resident involvement in neighborhood politics, whereby residents involve themselves to rid the community of problems that concern them but disappear once the problems are solved or ameliorated.

HILLTOP

> Some people say that the Hilltop is feisty. I don't think so. We are just concerned about our neighborhood. People also have a tendency to look down on the Hilltop, but they should not. It is up and coming.[7]

The low-poverty neighborhoods selected for the study are the predominantly white Hilltop and the predominantly black North Central neighborhoods. Interestingly, the Franklinton and Hilltop communities have similar beginnings. Lucus Sullivant, the founder of Franklinton, was the first settler to arrive in the Hilltop area (Daft 1979). While he resided in Franklinton, his two sons—William and Michael—lived at Hilltop, at what was formerly known as Sullivant's Hill. The growth of Franklinton in the mid-nineteenth century as well as the expansion of the railroads led to a slow but steady increase in the number of Hilltop residents. However, unlike Franklinton, Hilltop's early development can be characterized as rural.

Franklinton's misfortune proved to be Hilltop's gain as the flood of 1913 spurred growth in the neighborhood, where people moved in search of higher ground (Daft 1979). Hilltop grew into a tight-knit community that was spotted with thriving businesses. It served as a training ground for a number of important political officials. By the mid-1950s, however, suburbanization and the development of shopping centers like Westland and Great Western as well as the construction of the outer-belt pulled prosperous and stable families out of Hilltop into suburban communities (Urban Land Institute 1992). Soon merchants and businesses closed as they were left without patrons.

According to a recent study of Hilltop, housing conditions range from moderate to poor and declining, although good housing stock can be found in some areas. The houses are predominantly one and two-story single-family dwellings, and over 50% are owner occupied. Hilltop is also home to some multi-family units (Urban Land Institute 1992).

Although concentrated commercial activity can be found in Hilltop along Broad and Sullivant Avenues, it is evident that these commercial arteries are in serious decline. The lack of on-street parking and surface parking also poses a problem for the viability of businesses along these arteries. A number of problems plague the Hilltop community. Chief among them is the deterioration of its housing stock, the poor maintenance of rental properties, and the deterioration of the infrastructure and commercial arteries.

However, the residents of the Hilltop community have not allowed these problems to deter them. According to Ms. Weaver, many residents of the Hilltop community are proud of their neighborhood and they are working hard to revitalize it. They have worked with city officials in an effort to secure Urban Land Infrastructure Recovery Project grants which will improve the substandard housing conditions of the community. Through the Envelope Program, residents are awarded 0% loans to fix the windows, doors and other aspects of their homes. Most importantly, the Hilltop community has engaged in efforts to revitalize their business community by securing matching loans for businesses who are interested in making capital improvements to their buildings. The commission has also secured money to fix sidewalks, curbing and lighting in the community.

Ms. Weaver noted that an important aspect of Hilltop Area Commission's success is its ability to work with political officials and to mobilize groups within the community. She noted that when the neighborhood decided to tackle crime, they organized small groups of community watch organizations which have reportedly deterred criminal behavior in the area. She said that the neighborhood is rich in older citizens who are active in the community and who have worked with the commission to find employment for the neighborhood youth. In the summer of 1997, the commission received a small grant, which allowed them to employ teenagers in neighborhood improvement projects. In this way, the neighborhood was able to solve the problem of teenage idleness and make a dent in efforts to beautify the community.

According to Ms. Weaver, the Hilltop Commission is successful because residents believe that it is not a "political" organization. Instead, many of the activities provide neighborhood residents with an opportunity to help themselves and help other people. Concern about the neighborhood was demonstrated in the efforts of neighborhood residents to remove a massage parlor from the community. According to Ms. Weaver, the neighborhood residents realized that it would have a negative influence on children, who had to walk by the parlor on the way to school. The area commission organized a protest of the business, which resulted in the owners closing the shop and moving from the Hilltop community three weeks after the protest by Hilltop residents.

Despite its situation of decline during the 1980s, Hilltop is currently being revitalized. The efforts of the neighborhood area commission have resulted in positive zoning developments, the construction of a new library as well as a new fire station. Over all, the growth of the community, especially with the targeted economic and commercial development suggests that the Hilltop neighborhood is one that, in the words of Ms. Weaver, is up and coming.

NORTH CENTRAL

> Our primary concern is the airport project. Other communities have managed to dissuade political officials that it should not be extended in the direction of their communities. If they extend it in the direction of our community, the market values of our homes will be decreased by 50%.[8]

The predominantly black North Central neighborhood shares South Linden's historical background (Urban Land Institute 1992). Like the other Columbus areas, it was initially settled by Revolutionary War soldiers, who received land grants for military service. Unlike South Linden, however, it was slowly developed and not annexed to the rest of the city until the 1960s. Additionally, the North Central neighborhood is primarily residential, with only segments of it containing small grocery stores and gas stations. There are no major food or clothing stores within its boundaries.

Although the commission is only two years old, residents are organized and currently waging a battle against proposed legislation to extend an airport runway in the direction of their community.[9] If the legislation is enacted, the construction of single-family homes will be prohibited and current homes will be devalued as much as 50%, as the deeds will be stamped to reflect a noise-hazard area.

Although the concentrated poverty and low poverty neighborhoods, respectively, share similar economic circumstances, leaders in the predominantly white neighborhoods of Franklinton and Hilltop have much more access to the policy-making process than their counterparts in the predominantly black neighborhoods of South Linden and North Central. The analyses chapters will allow for an examination of the implications of this unequal access for the political behavior of inner-city residents.

SELECTION OF RESPONDENTS

Respondents for the study were randomly selected within each of the neighborhoods using a criss-cross directory. The birthday method was used to randomly select an adult within the household.[10] Also, in an effort to minimize race effects, white interviewers called on the predominantly white concentrated poverty and low poverty neighborhoods, while black callers interviewed respondents of predominantly black concentrated poverty and low poverty neighborhoods.

The telephone survey lasted 20 minutes each and produced 1,165 completed interviews, with 432 respondents from the predominantly black concentrated poverty neighborhood, 327 from the predominantly white concentrated poverty neighborhood, 205 from the predominantly black low poverty neighborhood and 201 from the predominantly white low poverty neighborhood.

THE QUESTIONNAIRE

In an effort to assess the impact of social contexts on the political participation of inner-city residents, the questionnaire included a wide array of questions. The proverbial net was cast rather broadly to include a wide range of political participation activities, political orientations and neighborhood orientations. In addition to these questions, respondents were asked about the participation habits of household members and the extent to which they were encouraged to participate in political activity by someone at home, at work, in the neighborhood and at church. Respondents were also queried about their involvement in social organizations as well as their religious affiliations. The survey questionnaire also explored the economic situations of respondents to determine whether or not they were able to purchase all of the things they needed, if they had to seek additional employment to make ends meet and whether or not the previous year's economic policies had an adverse impact on their personal economic situation. In addition to the usual demographic questions that are posed at the end of survey questionnaires, respondents were asked detailed questions about their households, including the extent to which household members received government benefits and the extent to which they owned basic resources like a home and an automobile.

The data set, which is being utilized in this study, presents a unique opportunity to examine the political behavior of white and black residents as influenced by inner-city social contexts. In the chapters that follow, the data are employed to test for racial differences in contextual effects (Chapter Four); variations in social isolation as a function of social context (Chapter Five); influence of neighborhood context on political behavior (Chapter Six); influence of family context on economic marginalization and political behavior (Chapter Seven); and the simultaneous direct and indirect influences of various social contexts on political behavior (Chapter Eight).

NOTES

1. Using census tracts as the initial indicator of neighborhood boundaries is a frequently utilized tactic in contextual research (Huckfeldt 1986; Giles, Wright and Dantico 1981).

2. Interview with Helen Evans, a member of the Franklinton Area Commission, July 1997.

3. Interview with Carol Stewart, a member and former chairperson of the Franklinton Area Commission, February 1993.

4. Interview with Clarence Lumpkin, founding member and former chairperson of the South Linden Area Commission, February 1993.

5. Interview with Clarence Lumpkin, founding member and former chairperson of the South Linden Area Commission, February 1993.

6. Interview with Clarence Lumpkin, former chairperson and founding member of the South Linden Area Commission, February 1993.

7. Interview with Pam Weaver, a member of the Hilltop Area Commission, July 1997.

8. Interview with Gloria Dubenion, secretary of the North Central Area Commission, February 1993.

9. Interview with Gloria Dubenion, secretary of the North Central Area Commission, February 1993.

10. Results from the pre-test phase of the survey, which used the Kitsch method of sampling, revealed that the sampled population was very sensitive when answering questions about household composition. Therefore, we utilized the birthday method which was less threatening and invasive than the Kitsch method, which requires respondents to indicate the number of individuals living in the household.

CHAPTER 4

Ghetto-Specific Behaviors in Black and White[1]

Now I am perfectly aware that there are other slums in which white men are fighting for their lives, and mainly losing. I know that blood is also flowing through those streets and that the human damage there is incalculable. People are continually pointing out to me the wretchedness of white people in order to console me for the wretchedness of blacks. But an itemized account of the American failure does not console me and it should not console anyone else.
James Baldwin 1960, *Nobody Knows My Name*

INTRODUCTION

As the foregoing quotation suggests, the issue of race has historically played an important and often controversial role in most contemporary debates about urban poverty (Banfield 1970; Murray 1984; Mead 1992; Wilson 1987). Some scholars argue that inner-city residents are predisposed to so-called ghetto or aberrant behaviors as a result of racial-cum-cultural factors (Murray 1984; Mead 1992). Others argue that while blacks are disproportionately represented among the population of residents in concentrated poverty inner-city communities, their plight is the result of debilitating structural factors but not the result of inherent racial traits or characteristics (Wilson 1987, 1996; Massey and Denton 1993).

Unfortunately, a lack of adequate data has made it impossible for urban poverty scholars to assess the extent to which socially aberrant behaviors, which are normally identified as race-specific, are also identifiable among poor whites who live in concentrated poverty neighborhoods. However, an increase in concentrated poverty neighborhoods predominated by whites has occasioned the opportunity to examine whether or not these so-called underclass behaviors or social pathologies emanate from concentrated poverty neighborhoods predominated by whites as well as blacks. After all, if the urban poverty problem is structural in nature, then whites and blacks in similar social contexts should exhibit similar levels of social pathologies. Toward that end, Chapter Four assesses the extent to which there are statistically significant differences in the behaviors of poor whites and blacks in concentrated poverty neighborhoods.

Indeed, the analysis is important in a number of respects. First, if racial factors are important in explaining the behaviors of inner-city residents, then ameliorative urban policies should have a racial thrust. Such evidence would also call into question the claim that blacks have unfettered access to social and economic resources, and that they should no longer cling to special protection benefits like affirmative action. Conversely, if the findings show a lack of racial differences between white and black residents of concentrated poverty neighborhoods, they would lend credence to structural arguments of urban poverty, which posit that contextual factors are more important than racial factors in explaining the behaviors of inner-city residents. Such findings would also lend support to race-neutral affirmative action policies which address income and structural shortcomings as opposed to racial inequities.

CONCENTRATED POVERTY AND RACE-SPECIFIC BEHAVIOR

Building on previous research on the concentrated poverty communities, this chapter assesses six characteristics that are traditionally associated with poor blacks in inner-city, concentrated poverty communities, including joblessness, welfare dependence, single-parent households, neighborhood criminal activity, civil disobedience/rioting, and social isolation.[2] These indicators have been utilized by both liberal and conservative scholars. The important difference is that conservative scholars have envisioned underclass behaviors and social welfare programs as primary causal agents of chronic poverty and the emergence of concentrated poverty neighborhoods (Murray 1984). On the other hand, liberal scholars have argued that underclass behavioral characteristics are a function of the social and economic isolation of concentrated poverty communities.

Employment Status: Joblessness is often considered a major cultural-cum-racially specific trait of blacks in inner-city communities. While some poverty scholars argue that the new urban poverty is a consequence of the dearth of available jobs which pay a living wage (Wilson 1987; Wilson and Wacquant 1989; Wacquant 1996; Jennings 1994), others contend the new urban poverty is the result of inner-city residents who lack the willingness to work (Mead 1986, 1992), a culture of dependence (Lemann 1991), and perverse government incentives (Murray 1984). If joblessness is race-specific, then poor whites should report significantly higher levels of employment than their poor black counterparts.

Welfare Dependence

Among recent theories of urban poverty, welfare dependence is often perceived as the major causal factor for the concentration of poverty among inner-city residents. One camp of scholars argues that a liberal welfare state has facilitated a perverse system of incentives which has made it more profitable to remain on the public dole than to work (Murray 1984; Mead 1986). If welfare dependence is driven by a mixture of cultural-cum-racial traits and perverse government incentives, then poor whites in concentrated poverty neighborhoods should report significantly lower levels of dependence on welfare benefits than their black counterparts.

Single-Parent Households

Since Moynihan's report on the black family, the problem of single-parent households has been viewed as an important defining characteristic of the black community. This study examines the extent to which there are racial differences according to family structure. If, as cultural theorists argue, blacks are culturally predisposed to form single-parent households, then the incidence of this type of family structure should be significantly lower among poor whites in concentrated poverty neighborhoods.

Neighborhood Criminal Activity

Concentrated poverty neighborhoods predominated by blacks are also notorious for either high levels of criminal activity or the perception that criminal activity is problematic. While the data set does not include actual crime statistics, it does evaluate residents' perceptions about neighborhood criminal activity, especially with respect to drugs and theft. If neighborhood criminal activity is race-specific, then reports of criminal activity should vary significantly between poor white and black residents of concentrated poverty communities.

Civil Disobedience

Predominantly black inner-city neighborhoods have also been historically associated with civil disobedience tactics as well as rioting as a means of affecting the public policy process. This analysis assesses the extent to which civil disobedience tactics emanate from racial proclivities or from structural factors like the spatial isolation of concentrated poverty neighborhoods.

Social Isolation

Social isolation is deemed by many structuralist interpretators of urban poverty as the mechanism by which the debilitating effects of urban social contexts influence behavior. Much of the urban poverty research suggests that blacks are uniquely crippled by social isolation as it stymies economic, social and political mobility. This chapter analyzes two components of social isolation. The first is the lack of upwardly mobile individuals in neighborhoods, generally known as the presence of role models. The second taps the reported level of involvement with religious and civic organizations. If blacks are uniquely socially isolated, then they should report significantly lower levels of organizational involvement than their white counterparts. The lack of role models should be more problematic among poor blacks than whites, especially as structural theories consider social isolation to be a problem that particularly plagues black people.

Table 4.1 provides a list of the concepts and their operationalizations.

Table 4.1

Concepts and Operationalizations

Concepts	Operationalizations
Employment Status	Included three categories: employed, unemployed and ineligible for employment (housewives, disabled persons, and full-time college students).
Welfare Dependence	Scale of means-tested benefits, including Aid to Families with Dependent Children (AFDC), housing subsidies, food stamps, and Medicaid. The scale ranged from 0 to 4, with 4 representing the highest level.
Family Structure	Included six categories: married with children, married without children, unmarried with children, unmarried without children, never married with children, and never married without children.
Neighborhood Criminal Activity	Residents' perceptions of problems with two types of crime: theft and drug activity.
Civil Disobedience	Whether or not respondents approved of protesting, disobeying a law, rioting to influence government policy-making.
Social Isolation	Measured in terms of the lack of role models and lack of involvement in civic and religious organizations.

METHODOLOGY

Concentrated poverty neighborhoods are comprised of both poor and nonpoor individuals. The first step in the analysis was to separate the poor residents from the nonpoor residents in both the predominantly black and predominantly white concentrated poverty neighborhoods. This yielded a sample of 318 poor respondents in concentrated poverty neighborhoods. Individuals who reported receiving less than $10,000 per year in income were characterized as poor, while individuals who received incomes above $10,000 were characterized as nonpoor.

Examined is the extent to which poor whites and blacks who live in separate concentrated poverty neighborhoods share socially aberrant traits which are normally used to characterize poor blacks. Chi-square tests were utilized to assess the extent to which the incidence of behaviors and characteristics was statistically different in the two neighborhoods.

FINDINGS

Tables 4.2–4.7 delineate the results of the bivariate analyses. The South Linden neighborhood is predominantly comprised of blacks, while the Franklinton neighborhood is predominantly comprised of whites.

Joblessness

As Table 4.2 depicts, the problem of joblessness is no stranger to either poor blacks or poor whites in concentrated poverty neighborhoods. In the predominantly African American neighborhood of South Linden, 40% of the residents were unemployed; 24% reported that they were ineligible for employment because they were disabled, students or homemakers, and 36% reported having either a full-time or part-time job. In Franklinton, 32% of the residents reported being unemployed; 31% stated that they were ineligible for employment and 37% reported that they were employed either full time or part time. The lack of viable employment opportunities and inadequate job network systems have combined to create bleak employment opportunities for South Linden and Franklinton residents.

While some researchers have contended that inner-city poverty stems from individual character flaws and deviant cultural values that predispose African Americans to choose not to work, the data show that the specter of unemployment is not merely an African American problem. Instead, research has shown that the high level of inner-city unemployment is a result of spatial mismatch of low-skilled employment opportunities (Kasarda 1992; Huges 1989) and dramatic changes in the labor market (Wilson 1987), which have affected all poorly skilled and undereducated inner-city residents since 1970, regardless of race (Kasarda 1985, 1989, 1992).

Welfare Dependence

According to poverty scholars, a primary behavioral characteristic of the urban underclass is dependence on government assistance (Wilson 1987; Mead 1992; Lemann 1986a, 1986b, 1991; Murray 1984). Although Aid to Families with Dependent Children (AFDC) is the most popular need-based benefit, there are other forms of assistance— namely housing subsidies, food stamps, and Medicaid—which are frequently distributed in concentrated poverty neighborhoods; they are therefore analyzed in this research study.

Table 4.2

Joblessness in South Linden and Franklinton

Response	South Linden	Franklinton
Employed	36%	37%
Unemployed	40%	32%
Ineligible for Employment	24%	31%
Total	100%	100%
N	127	100
Chi-Square = 2.16		
Probability = .339		

Source: 1991 Columbus Neighborhood Study Data Set.

Table 4.3

Means-Tested Public Assistance in South Linden and Franklinton

Response	South Linden	Franklinton
No assistance	38%	51%
One subsidy	24%	17%
Two subsidies	15%	13%
Three subsidies	17%	16%
Four subsidies	6%	3%
Total	100%	100%
N	178	133
Chi-Square = .308		
Probability = .579		

Source: 1991 Columbus Neighborhood Study Data Set.

As a result, because of the low percentages of employed people in Franklinton and South Linden, it is not surprising that almost 50% of the residents in both communities receive some form of means-tested government aid. In contrast to what Mead (1992) and Murray (1984) have suggested in their studies, the chi-square test reveals that poor whites in concentrated poverty neighborhoods are just as likely as their poor African American counterparts to be dependent on government assistance in the form of AFDC, subsidized public housing, food stamps and Medicaid. If an innate sense of defeatism (Mead 1992) and *get over mentality* (Lemann 1986a, 1986b) accounts for the dependency of African Americans on government assistance, then one has to wonder about the reasons for a similar pattern among poor whites.

Family Structure

Apart from the concentrated poverty neighborhoods being viewed in terms of low employment rates and welfare dependence, they are also frequently associated with high concentrations of single-parent households. Since the well known Moynihan Report (Moynihan 1965), utilizing family structure as an indicator of underclass or ghetto behavior has been known to generate controversy. Underlying this concept is not only a preoccupation with so-called aberrant African American culture that has deviated from the two-parent, nuclear family structure (Loury 1985; Mead 1992) but also an empirically based understanding that economic hardship is often synonymous with female-headed families (McLanahan 1995).

In one respect, the findings shown in Table 4.4 do substantiate the claims of Wilson (1987) and others with regard to family structure. For example, only 12% of families in South Linden and 16% of families in Franklinton happened to be two-parent households. However, a statistically significant chi-square suggests that the family structures in South Linden and Franklinton are qualitatively different. Poor African Americans are more likely to experience marital disruption than their poor white counterparts. Furthermore, differences have also emerged among those who reported that they had never been married. Residents in the predominantly black concentrated poverty neighborhood of South Linden were almost three times more likely to report that they had never been married but had children (20%); whites in the concentrated poverty neighborhood of Franklinton were two times more likely to report that they had never been married and had no children (33%).

Although these racial differences are interesting, the most surprising finding is that the largest percentages of households in South Linden (44%) and the second largest in Franklinton (32%) are composed of unmarried women with children. It is, therefore, important to underscore that these women were once married, but marital dissolution occurred as a result of separation, divorce or death. Consequently, single-parent households are not predominantly the result of unwed mothers who have chosen not to marry because of

Table 4.4
Family Structure in South Linden and Franklinton

Response	South Linden	Franklinton
Married with children	12%	16%
Married without children	1%	3%
Unmarried with children	44%	32%
Unmarried without children	9%	9%
Never married with children	20%	7%
Never married without children	14%	33%
Total	100%	100%
N	178	133
Chi-Square = 18.301		
Probability = .003		

Source: 1991 Columbus Neighborhood Study Data Set.

Table 4.5
Criminal Activity in South Linden and Franklinton

Response	South Linden	Franklinton
Illegal drug activity		
Big problem	70%	64%
Somewhat of a problem/ no problem	30%	36%
Total	100%	100%
N	167	116
Chi-Square = .996		
Probability = .318		
Theft and burglary		
Big problem	61%	61%
Somewhat of a problem/ no problem	39%	39%
Total	100%	100%
N	169	127
Chi-Square = .006		
Probability = .934		

Source: 1991 Columbus Neighborhood Study Data Set.

perverse or easy-to-come by government incentives as Murray (1984) suggested, or because of autonomous, aberrant social norms and values, as Lemann (1986a, 1986b, 1991) and Mead (1992) suggested. Nor are they solely the result of unemployment among black men as Wilson (1987) suggested. Instead, the data in this study indicate that the prevalence of single-parent households is largely a result of failed marriages, a phenomenon that is not exclusive to neighborhoods predominated by poor African Americans but one that has resonated generally across the American population.

Criminal Activity

Studies of concentrated poverty neighborhoods have suggested that low educational attainment, welfare dependency, and the lack of employment opportunities are all related to high levels of neighborhood criminal activity (Sampson 1987). Although crime statistics were not collected for these areas, the data set does include questions about residents' perceptions of problems with neighborhood drug activity and thefts. As the chi-square statistics in Table 4.5 reveal, the concentrated poverty communities of Franklinton and South Linden do not differ statistically in this matter; residents in both neighborhoods have reported respective problems with neighborhood crime. Of the two community crime problems sampled in this study, residents in both neighborhoods identified drug activity as the most troublesome. This finding is especially interesting as the drug problem has often been cast as a black (or minority) problem.

Civil Disobedience and Rioting

Crime is not only associated with predominantly black inner-city neighborhoods, but with aggressive political tactics like rioting and other forms of civil disobedience. However, there is very little evidence about the extent to which whites in concentrated poverty neighborhoods engage in similar activities. After all, it is expected that residents of low poverty neighborhoods are less likely than residents in concentrated poverty neighborhoods to involve themselves in civil disobedience tactics to express their political views. These assumptions were borne out in the 1960s Watts Riots as well as the multi-city riots of 1992 in the wake of the Rodney King beating and its court verdict. However, the results revealed that blacks and poor whites in impoverished neighborhood contexts do not differ dramatically in their

Table 4.6
Civil Disobedience Tactics in South Linden and Franklinton

Responses	South Linden	Franklinton
Refuse to obey a law		
Approve	37%	41%
Disapprove	63%	59%
Total	100%	100%
N	150	110
Chi-Square = .482		
Probability = .487		
Stop government with sit-ins, demonstrations		
Approve	43%	40%
Disapprove	57%	60%
Total	100%	100%
N	149	119
Chi-Square = .186		
Probability = .666		
Stop government with rioting		
Approve	30%	22%
Disapprove	70%	78%
Total	100%	100%
N	156	123
Chi-Square = 2.02		
Probability = .155		

Source: 1991 Columbus Neighborhood Study Data Set.

approval of civil disobedience tactics. In fact, the findings delineated in Table 4.6 reveal wide levels of agreement among whites and blacks in their approval of civil disobedience tactics. Almost 40% of poor blacks and whites reported that they approved of refusing to obey unjust laws and of stopping government with protests and sit-in demonstrations. Similarly, approximately 25% of poor blacks and whites approved of stopping government with rioting. These findings are highly important in light of the recent Los Angeles and Miami County uprisings. They suggest that whites caught in concentrated poverty neighborhoods and poverty are just as likely to approve of civil disobedience tactics as their black counterparts.

Social Isolation

In addition to theorizing about the aforementioned ghetto-specific behaviors and attributes, urban poverty scholars (Wilson 1987; Massey and Denton 1993) also bemoaned the lack of neighborhood role models in concentrated poverty neighborhoods. They suggested that the exodus of middle- and working-class families from concentrated poverty neighborhoods has adversely contributed to the concentration of poor people in inner-city neighborhoods. Undesirable behaviors have emanated from concentrated poverty neighborhoods because residents are out of touch with mainstream role models who have moved to other neighborhoods (Wilson 1987). Although Wilson suggested that the problem of social isolation is confined to the African American community—and specifically to African Americans in concentrated poverty neighborhoods—the findings have also shown that whites in concentrated poverty communities report high levels of social isolation. When asked if role models lived in their neighborhoods, 71% of poor whites, as compared with 59% of poor blacks, reported that role models lived in other neighborhoods. Consequently, these findings have suggested that the exodus of middle- and working-class families is not necessarily a black phenomenon but one that has affected concentrated poverty neighborhoods in general. The statistically significant chi square suggests that these differences are statistically and substantively important.

Wilson has also argued that concentrated poverty neighborhoods lack the social network systems of association that normally facilitate strong community organizations. His thesis is substantiated, in part, by the data in Table 4.7. In comparing the attendance of poor whites and poor blacks at religious services, poor whites are much less likely than their black counterparts to report regular church attendance. As compared with 64% of poor blacks, who report going to church services several times a week, 37% of poor whites said that they attend church several times a week. Additionally, blacks are more likely to be involved in organizations than their white counterparts. Almost 40% of poor whites reported that they did not belong to a single

Table 4.7
Social Isolation in South Linden and Franklinton

Responses	South Linden	Franklinton
Upwardly mobile individuals live		
In my neighborhood	41%	29%
Elsewhere	59%	71%
Total	100%	100%
N	156	106
Chi-Square = 3.78		
Probability = .051		
How frequently do you attend religious services		
Never	6%	20%
Several times a year	10%	25%
Monthly	20%	18%
Several times a week	64%	37%
Total	100%	100%
N	164	114
Chi-Square = .29.77		
Probability = .000		
Organizational membership		
None	22%	39%
One or more	78%	61%
Total	100%	100%
N	178	133
Chi-Square = 7.20		
Probability = .125		

Source: 1991 Columbus Neighborhood Study Data Set.

organization, compared with about 20% of poor blacks. The statistically significant chi square for organizational membership and religious attendance suggests that these differences are substantively and statistically significant.

SOCIALLY ABERRANT BEHAVIORS ARE NOT RACE-SPECIFIC

Poor whites are usually not included in urban poverty discussions and debates, but the findings of Chapter Four suggest that they should be included in future discussions for various reasons including policy geared toward ameliorating the plight of socially and spatially isolated inner-city residents. The data show not only that poor whites in concentrated poverty neighborhoods are on par with poor blacks in terms of joblessness, welfare dependence, the perception of criminal activity, unemployment, approval of civil disobedience tactics, but also that poor whites in concentrated poverty neighborhoods are even more disconnected than their poor black counterparts from the broader society as evinced by the relative lack of role models and involvement in social and religious institutions. These findings are important in illuminating the relevance of neighborhood social contexts as poor whites and blacks in different concentrated poverty neighborhoods exhibit similar levels of what is commonly known as ghetto-specific behaviors, despite racial differences.

While Chapter Four's findings are important in facilitating an understanding of how neighborhood social contexts influence behaviors among poor whites and blacks, it is also necessary to understand the extent to which concentrated poverty neighborhoods engender social isolation. It is to this query that we now turn in Chapter Five.

NOTES

1. This chapter is based on Yvette Alex-Assensoh, "Myths About Race and the Underclass: Concentrated Poverty and 'Underclass' Behaviors." *Urban Affairs Review*. 31 (1): 3–19.

2. A questionnaire utilized in this analysis is presented in Appendix A.

CHAPTER 5

Neighborhood Poverty and Social Isolation in Inner-City America

INTRODUCTION

Considered the theoretical linchpin of structural theories of urban poverty, social isolation is the concept that is utilized to explain the behavior of individual inner-city residents who have been affected by the macro-level restructuring in the economy (Fernandez and Harris 1992). According to structuralists, social isolation is the mechanism through which the debilitating influences of inner-city social contexts affect the behavior of inner-city residents (Wilson 1987; Wilson and Wacquant 1989; Harrell and Peterson 1992). Furthermore, it is the marked spatial isolation of concentrated poverty neighborhoods and the subsequent social isolation of residents which allegedly distinguish the new " urban poverty" (Wilson 1996; Massey and Denton 1993) from earlier historical incidents of impoverishment and neighborhood ghettoization (Wilson 1987).

The model of political participation, as specified in Chapter Two, posits that social isolation also has important consequences for political participation. Indeed, it is very difficult for residents to affect public policy if they are isolated from social networks, social or political organizations and local government by virtue of debilitating neighborhood contexts. After all, the spatial concentration and social isolation of inner-city residents particularizes their needs and makes it more difficult to engage in coalitional activities (Massey and Denton 1993). This phenomenon is evident in the chronic problems of inadequate schools and city services which disproportionately affect poor residents in concentrated poverty neighborhoods. Middle-class individuals, who frequently reside in more socially integrated neighborhoods, do not have the urgent and pressing concerns about school safety and educational reform of many inner-city residents. Therefore, residents in inner-city communities often find themselves standing alone in metropolitan-wide discussions of financial priorities and educational policies. Toward these ends, the goal of this chapter is to assess the extent to which residence in concentrated poverty neighborhoods leads to social isolation.

INDICATORS AND CORRELATES OF SOCIAL ISOLATION

The concept of social isolation has been defined in myriad ways, but most credible conceptualizations and operationalizations of the term focus on the absence of interaction with individuals and institutions in the mainstream of society. Among current studies of urban poverty, the concept of social isolation has come to represent the absence of upwardly mobile individuals who once served as role models and social buffers (Wilson 1987).

In this chapter, six different indicators of social isolation are utilized to assess whether or not individuals in concentrated poverty neighborhoods are more likely to exhibit signs of social isolation once variations in individual income and race are controlled. In keeping with the urban poverty literature, the indicators and correlates of social isolation—which are utilized in this chapter—include economic marginalization, poor neighborhood services, high levels of criminal activity, limited social networks and lack of involvement with social and religious institutions and organizations.

Economic Marginalization

Residence in concentrated poverty neighborhoods is expected to worsen the economic plight of poor individuals. Geographic isolation from the economic and social heart of urban communities makes it difficult to find suitable and accessible employment. Moreover, the deterioration of concentrated poverty neighborhoods often dissuades new businesses from locating in inner-city areas, while the poverty of community residents compels existing businesses to relocate to more prosperous areas within the city or surrounding suburban areas. It is hypothesized that white and black residents in concentrated poverty neighborhoods will be more likely to report joblessness and dependence on government aid. Also, residents of concentrated poverty neighborhoods are expected to be less likely to own homes and cars, resources that are considered as basic necessities for many Americans.

Poor Neighborhood Services

Residence in concentrated poverty neighborhoods is also expected to correlate with lower levels of satisfaction with neighborhood services and resources. Largely comprised of impoverished individuals, concentrated poverty neighborhoods are less likely than low poverty neighborhoods to be embedded in socio-political networks that address issues of neighborhood deterioration. Moreover, since these communities are often located outside the parameters of the business and downtown sectors, politicians have no inherent political need to ensure that concentrated poverty neighborhoods are as well maintained as their working- and middle-class counterparts. Neighborhood services are expected to be especially problematic in the areas of garbage collection and shopping resources.

Criminal Activity

The lack of connection with mainstream institutions is also expected to manifest itself in higher levels of criminal activity and perceptions of the same for residents in concentrated poverty neighborhoods. The geographic isolation of concentrated poverty communities as well as the concentration of impoverished individuals combine to make it an ideal location for criminal activity because of the impoverished plight of the residents and the inattentiveness of public officials. Characteristic of this phenomenon is the crack epidemic, which has gripped many inner-city communities across the United States. Compared to residents in low poverty neighborhoods, the residents in concentrated poverty neighborhoods are expected to be more likely to report problems with drug activities as well as problems with theft and burglary in their neighborhood (Fernandez and Harris 1992; Rose and McClain 1990).

Social Networks

Underlying the emphasis on role models and the lack of middle-class presence in concentrated poverty neighborhoods is the implication that social communication has important consequences for the social, economic and political behavior of inner-city residents. After all, numerous studies have underscored the importance of social networking on employment outcomes, indicating that employment opportunities often come about as a result of informal networking (Kirschenman and Neckerman 1991; Jencks and Peterson 1991; Wilson 1987, 1996). Therefore, it is not surprising that inner-city residents, who live in concentrated poverty neighborhoods that have a dearth of upwardly mobile role models, are frequently more jobless than their counterparts in low poverty neighborhoods. Research has also indicated that the friendship networks of individuals in concentrated poverty neighborhoods are also more concentrated, which is indicative of a smaller range of network associations (Wilson and Wacquant 1989).

Lack of Involvement with Organizations/Institutions

A particularly foreboding characterization of concentrated poverty communities suggests that they are devoid of viable social institutions as a result of the deconcentration of middle-class families (Jencks and Peterson 1991). Religious organizations, especially churches, reportedly constitute the last of the remaining organizations in such neighborhoods. Institutions and organizations are important to the extent that they facilitate inter-class interaction and serve as a foray into participation with the broader society. Therefore, the absence of viable institutions from concentrated poverty communities constitutes a serious handicap and problem for political participation. Residents in concentrated poverty neighborhoods are expected to report less involvement in such institutions than their counterparts in low poverty neighborhoods.

Undergirded by the research discussed above, this chapter assesses the impact of residence in concentrated poverty neighborhoods on four indicators and correlates of social isolation. Table 5.1 delineates the concepts and operationalizations that will be utilized.

METHODOLOGY

Gainsayers of contextual effects often claim that so-called contextual effects are merely spurious findings that are the result of inadequate controls at the individual level. However, this study has made the proper provisions to control for the effects of race and individual income, two variables that could possibly confound the results. In fact,

Table 5.1

Concepts and Operationalizations

Concepts	Operationalizations
Economic Marginalization	Measured the extent to which residents possess basic resources: owning an automobile, whether they rent or own a home, and whether they receive means-tested government benefits.
Neighborhood Services	Assessed how residents rated neighborhood city services and resources, including garbage collection and shopping centers.
Criminal Activity	Evaluated residents' perceptions of drug activity and theft in neighborhoods.
Social Networks	Whether neighborhood residents reported that upwardly mobile individuals lived in their neighborhood or some other neighborhoods; depth of social networks.
Lack of Involvement in Organizations and Institutions	Church attendance and membership in social organizations.

Table 5.2

Contingency Table Diagram

Neighborhood Context	Poor		Nonpoor	
	Black	White	Black	White
Concentrated Poverty				
Low Poverty				

it is the purpose of this chapter as well as the two subsequent chapters (Chapters Six and Seven) to determine whether or not the influences of social contexts at the family and neighborhood levels are important above and beyond the impact of individual characteristics.

If social contexts at the neighborhood and family levels have an independent influence on social isolation (Chapter Five), and political participation (Chapters Six and Seven), then the analyses should exhibit statistically significant differences in the dependent variables once variations in individual income and race are controlled. This should be evident for poor individuals in concentrated poverty and low poverty neighborhoods and nonpoor individuals in concentrated poverty and low poverty neighborhoods, respectively. To test these hypotheses, it was necessary to categorize respondents into one of eight groups, namely black and white poor people in concentrated poverty neighborhoods, black and white poor people in low poverty neighborhoods, black and white nonpoor people in concentrated poverty neighborhoods and black and white nonpoor people in low poverty neighborhoods. Neighborhoods where the poverty rate was 20% were characterized as low poverty neighborhoods, while those in which the poverty rate registered above 40% were characterized as concentrated poverty neighborhoods. An illustration of the comparisons that will be made in this Chapter as well as Chapters Six and Seven has been provided in Table 5.2.

ECONOMIC MARGINALIZATION

Figure 5.1 presents the results for economic marginalization among poor whites. Contrary to expectations, there are only two important substantive differences in economic marginalization between poor whites in concentrated poverty and low poverty neighborhoods. Poor whites in concentrated poverty neighborhoods are more likely to rent and much less likely to own an automobile than their counterparts in the low poverty neighborhood of Hilltop. While poor whites in concentrated poverty neighborhoods are also two times more likely than their counterparts in low poverty neighborhoods to receive AFDC, the relationship falls just short of statistical significance at the .05 level. Also, contrary to expectations is the small difference between the poor whites in concentrated poverty and low poverty neighborhoods in terms of receiving food stamps. The jobless rate among poor whites is low in both concentrated poverty and low poverty neighborhoods.

In contrast, nonpoor whites in concentrated poverty neighborhoods exhibit very telling signs of economic marginalization as compared with their counterparts in the low poverty neighborhoods. There are statistically significant differences with respect to home ownership, transportation and government benefits. As depicted in Figure 5.2, nonpoor whites in concentrated poverty communities are almost twice as likely as their counterparts in the low poverty

Figure 5.1:
Economic Marginalization among Poor Inner-City Whites: A Comparison of
Concentrated Poverty and Low Poverty Neighborhoods

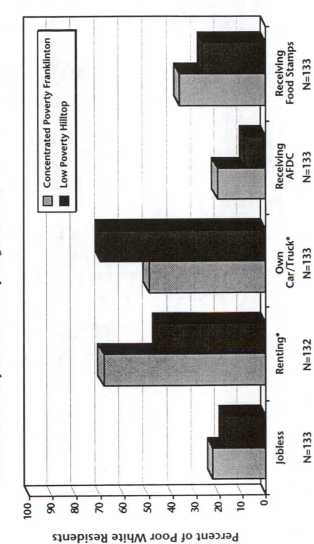

Source: 1991 Columbus Neighborhood Study Data Set.

*** $p \leq .001$; ** $p \leq .01$; * $p \leq .05$.

Figure 5.2:
Economic Marginalization among Non-poor Inner-City Whites: A Comparison of Concentrated Poverty and Low Poverty Neighborhoods

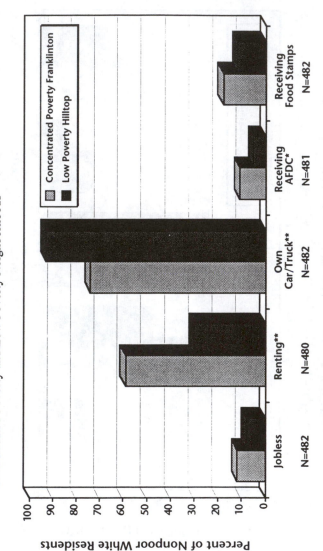

Source: 1991 Columbus Neighborhood Study Data Set.

*** $p \leq .001$; ** $p \leq .01$; * $p \leq .05$.

neighborhoods to rent. Residents in concentrated poverty neighborhoods are also considerably less likely to own automobiles, which are almost essential in today's decentralized labor market. Although the numbers of nonpoor whites receiving government benefits is low, compared with their poor counterparts, nonpoor whites in the concentrated poverty neighborhood are almost twice as likely to receive AFDC. However, the percentage of nonpoor whites, who receive food stamps, is low and the difference between residents of concentrated poverty and low poverty neighborhoods is small and statistically insignificant. Also, there is only a small difference in the joblessness rates of nonpoor residents in concentrated poverty and low poverty neighborhoods, and, compared to their poor counterparts, the percentages are quite small.

Among poor blacks, there is a great degree of economic marginalization among residents in concentrated poverty neighborhoods, vis-à-vis low poverty neighborhood residents (Figure 5.3). Compared with residents in low poverty areas, poor blacks in the concentrated poverty neighborhood are almost four times more likely to be jobless. Additionally, there is almost a 20% difference in car and home ownership between black residents in concentrated poverty and low poverty neighborhoods. Poor blacks in the concentrated poverty neighborhood are much more likely to rent and to report that they do not own an automobile than their counterparts in the low poverty North Central neighborhood. In light of the high level of joblessness, the stark differences in the degree of dependence on government assistance are not surprising. Poor Blacks in concentrated poverty neighborhoods are almost three times as likely to receive welfare and food stamps as their counterparts in low poverty neighborhoods.

The spatial isolation of concentrated poverty neighborhoods also exerts an important influence on the economic well-being of nonpoor blacks (Figure 5.4). As compared with nonpoor blacks in low poverty neighborhoods, their counterparts in concentrated poverty neighborhoods are almost four times more likely to be jobless, even though the jobless rate is relatively low as compared with their poor counterparts. It is not surprising, therefore, that almost five times as many nonpoor blacks in concentrated poverty neighborhoods as compared with low poverty neighborhoods receive AFDC, which is commonly known as welfare. Additionally, compared with 7% of nonpoor blacks in the low poverty neighborhood, 25% of blacks in concentrated poverty neighborhoods receive food stamps.

Figure 5.3:
Economic Marginalization among Poor Inner-City Blacks: A Comparison of
Concentrated Poverty and Low Poverty Neighborhoods

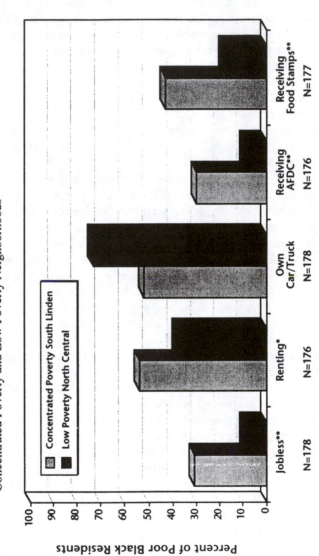

Source: 1991 Columbus Neighborhood Study Data Set.

*** $p \leq .001$; ** $p \leq .01$; * $p \leq .05$.

Figure 5.4:
Economic Marginalization among Non-poor Inner-City Blacks: A Comparison of
Concentrated Poverty and Low Poverty Neighborhoods

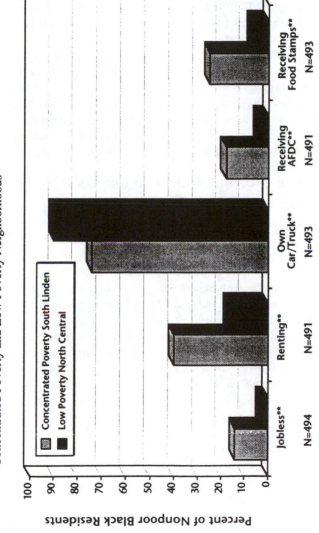

Source: 1991 Columbus Neighborhood Study Data Set.

*** $p \leq .001$; ** $p \leq .01$; * $p \leq .05$.

While many Americans take both home and car ownership as either a given or *sine qua non* of American life, almost 40% of nonpoor blacks in concentrated poverty neighborhoods reported that they do not own a car, compared with 17% in low poverty neighborhoods. Also, compared with a 90% automobile ownership rate in the low poverty neighborhood, 74% of working-class Blacks in concentrated poverty neighborhoods own cars.

The findings delineated in Figures 5.1, 5.2, 5.3 and 5.4 demonstrate the statistically significant relationship between residence in concentrated poverty neighborhoods and economic marginalization. These trends are evident among poor and nonpoor blacks and especially among nonpoor whites. The next section of the chapter assesses how residence in concentrated poverty neighborhoods impacts residents' perceptions of neighborhood services and criminal activity.

NEIGHBORHOOD SERVICES AND CRIMINAL ACTIVITY

The findings for neighborhood services and criminal activity among poor whites are presented in Figure 5.5. Satisfaction with neighborhood shopping is considerably high among poor white residents in concentrated poverty and low poverty neighborhoods; however, poor whites in concentrated poverty areas are less likely to express satisfaction with neighborhood shopping than their counterparts in the low poverty neighborhood.[1] Very few differences emerge with regard to garbage collection services, whereby a majority of poor white residents approve of these services. While poor whites in concentrated poverty neighborhoods were considerably more likely to report problems with drug activity in the neighborhood, theft was seen as problematic in both neighborhoods.

Nonpoor whites reported similar levels of high and moderate satisfaction with shopping facilities and garbage collection, respectively, regardless of neighborhood differences (Figure 5.6). While whites in both neighborhoods expressed serious concern about problems with theft in the neighborhood, nonpoor whites in concentrated poverty communities were more likely than their counterparts in low poverty neighborhoods to report that neighborhood residents had big problems with illegal drugs. Similar to the reports of drug activity delineated in Chapter Three, these findings suggest that drug activity is not a uniquely African American phenomenon. Instead, it is a scourge that threatens to annihilate white and black

Figure 5.5:
Neighborhood Services and Criminal Activity among Poor Inner-City Whites:
A Comparison of Concentrated Poverty and Low Poverty Neighborhoods

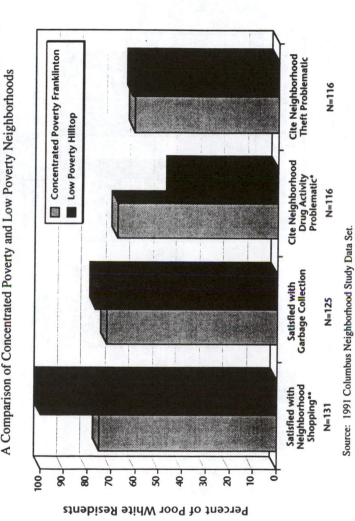

Source: 1991 Columbus Neighborhood Study Data Set.

*** $p \le .001$; ** $p \le .01$; * $p \le .05$.

Figure 5.6:
Neighborhood Services and Criminal Activity among Non-poor Inner-City Whites: A Comparison of Concentrated Poverty and Low Poverty Neighborhoods

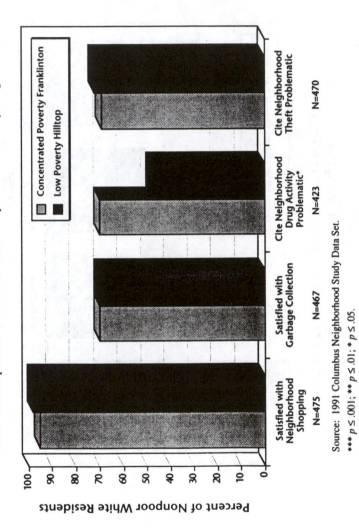

Source: 1991 Columbus Neighborhood Study Data Set.

*** $p \leq .001$; ** $p \leq .01$; * $p \leq .05$.

neighborhoods, alike, especially those that are mired in the web of inner-city poverty.

Consistent with expectations, poor blacks in concentrated poverty and low poverty neighborhoods reported different evaluations of neighborhood services (Figure 5.7). In concentrated poverty neighborhoods, poor blacks are less likely to report that they are satisfied with neighborhood shopping. Problems with crime are also evident among poor blacks. Residents of the concentrated poverty community are more likely to report that theft is a big neighborhood problem as compared with their counterparts in the low poverty neighborhood of North Central.

Neighborhood differences are also evident among nonpoor blacks (Figure 5.8). In low poverty neighborhoods, nonpoor blacks are more likely than their counterparts in concentrated poverty neighborhoods to express satisfaction with neighborhood shopping facilities and garbage collection. Consistent with the hypothesis that drug activity is more prevalent in concentrated poverty neighborhoods is the finding that almost 50% of the residents in concentrated poverty neighborhoods maintained that the neighborhood had a big problem with drugs. Theft, however, is a problem that plagues both concentrated poverty and low poverty neighborhoods.

Summarily, then, the findings lend credence to the hypothesis that residence in concentrated poverty neighborhoods correlates highly with criminal activity and poor neighborhood services. For example, drug activity was prevalent in concentrated poverty neighborhoods predominated by whites as well as blacks. With the exception of nonpoor whites, residents in concentrated poverty neighborhoods were more likely than their counterparts in low poverty neighborhoods to report dissatisfaction with neighborhood services.

The next section of the chapter examines the relationship between residence in concentrated poverty neighborhoods and access to important human capital resources.

ROLE MODELS AND INSTITUTIONAL INVOLVEMENT

While economic marginalization, neighborhood services and criminal activity are relevant correlates of social isolation, contemporary urban scholars argue that the lack of interaction with upwardly mobile individuals and institutions which represent mainstream society is the most viable measure of social isolation (Massey and Denton 1993;

Figure 5.7:
Neighborhood Services and Criminal Activity among Poor Inner-City Blacks:
A Comparison of Concentrated Poverty and Low Poverty Neighborhoods

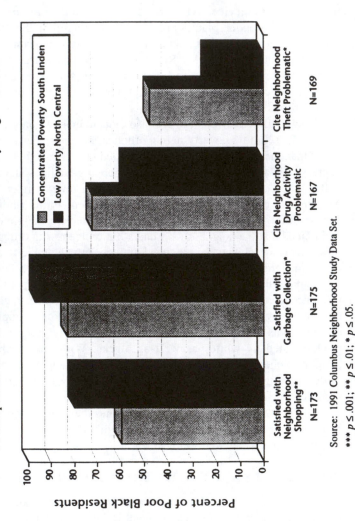

Source: 1991 Columbus Neighborhood Study Data Set.

*** $p \leq .001$; ** $p \leq .01$; * $p \leq .05$.

Figure 5.8:

Neighborhood Services and Criminal Activity among Non-poor Inner-City Blacks: A Comparison of Concentrated Poverty and Low Poverty Neighborhoods

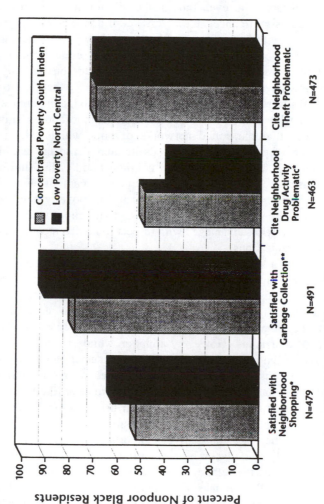

Source: 1991 Columbus Neighborhood Study Data Set.

*** $p \leq .001$; ** $p \leq .01$; * $p \leq .05$.

Wilson 1987). Toward that end, the final section of this chapter assesses the relationship between residence in concentrated poverty neighborhoods and access to role models and institutions.

Poor whites in concentrated poverty neighborhoods exhibited signs of social isolation, even though the relationships fell just short of statistical significance at the 95% confidence level (Figure 5.9). Compared with 53% of poor whites in the low poverty neighborhood, 74% of all interviewed residents of the concentrated poverty community reported a lack of role models. Additionally, only 55% of poor, low poverty neighborhood residents reported that their friendship networks were concentrated in the neighborhood, compared with 75% of poor whites in concentrated poverty neighborhoods. This pattern indicates that the social networks of poor whites who reside in concentrated poverty neighborhoods are more dense and less integrated beyond the confines of their neighborhood. The findings also demonstrated a small and statistically insignificant difference between poor whites in concentrated poverty and low poverty neighborhoods. Overall, however, they suggested that poor whites are not institutionally disadvantaged with respect to involvement in church and social organizations.

Nonpoor whites in concentrated poverty neighborhoods were also more likely to bemoan the lack of role models in their neighborhood, which is indicative of middle-class flight and the lack of inter-class interaction (Figure 5.10). However, they were no more likely than residents in the low poverty areas to report a limited or shallow social network of friends. However, nonpoor whites in the concentrated poverty neighborhoods reported less social interaction with mainstream institutions than their counterparts in low poverty neighborhoods. Whites in concentrated poverty areas were less likely to frequent church and more likely to refrain from organizational memberships than their counterparts in low poverty communities.

While there are substantively important differences in the social networks of poor blacks in concentrated poverty and low poverty neighborhoods, the relationships do not reach statistical significance (Figure 5.11). Poor Blacks in concentrated poverty neighborhoods are more likely to report that their area lacks upwardly mobile individuals who can serve as role models. They are also more likely to report shallow and limited friendship networks. These findings indicate that poor blacks in concentrated poverty neighborhoods are much less likely to interact with middle-class individuals and that their friendship

Figure 5.9:
Lack of Role Models and Institutional Involvement among Poor Inner-City
Whites: A Comparison of Concentrated Poverty and Low Poverty Neighborhoods

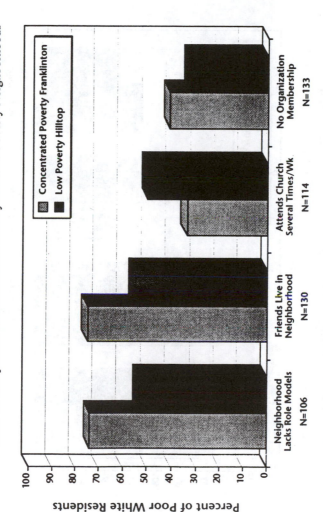

Source: 1991 Columbus Neighborhood Study Data Set.

*** $p \leq .001$; ** $p \leq .01$; * $p \leq .05$.

Figure 5.10:
Lack of Role Models and Institutional Involvement among Non-poor Inner-City
Whites: A Comparison of Concentrated Poverty and Low Poverty Neighborhoods

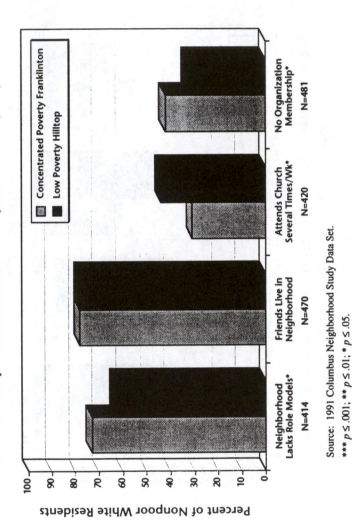

Source: 1991 Columbus Neighborhood Study Data Set.

*** $p \le .001$; ** $p \le .01$; * $p \le .05$.

Figure 5.11:
Lack of Role Models and Institutional Involvement among Poor Inner-City Blacks: A Comparison of Concentrated Poverty and Low Poverty Neighborhoods

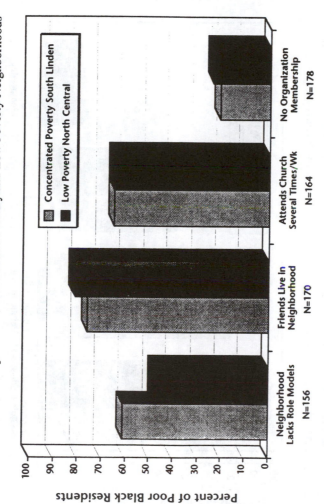

Source: 1991 Columbus Neighborhood Study Data Set.

*** $p \leq .001$; ** $p \leq .01$; * $p \leq .05$.

Figure 5.12:
Lack of Role Models and Institutional Involvement among Non-poor Inner-City
Blacks: A Comparison of Concentrated Poverty and Low Poverty Neighborhoods

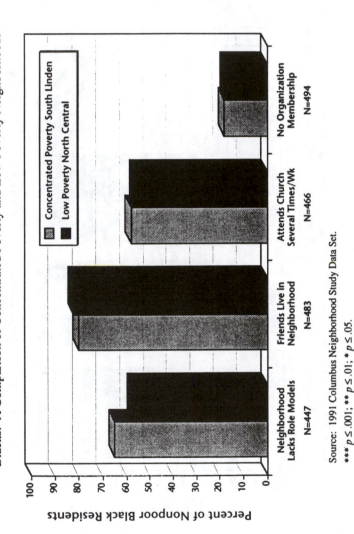

Source: 1991 Columbus Neighborhood Study Data Set.

*** $p \le .001$; ** $p \le .01$; * $p \le .05$.

networks are more concentrated than their counterparts in low poverty neighborhoods.

Contrary to expectations, there are very few differences in institutional involvement between poor blacks in concentrated poverty and low poverty neighborhoods. Instead, the findings reveal that regardless of differences in the social contexts of their neighborhoods poor blacks reported high levels of involvement in church and social organizations.

No substantively or statistically significant differences were evident in either the social interaction or institutional involvement of nonpoor blacks (Figure 5.12). Instead, blacks in concentrated poverty neighborhoods and low poverty neighborhoods reported healthy levels of involvement in social and religious organizations.

SUMMARY AND DISCUSSION

The findings present a varied and differentiated assessment of social isolation as a consequence of residence in inner-city concentrated poverty neighborhoods. The findings were extremely important in demonstrating that contextual factors play a large role in economic marginalization and that the likelihood of receiving government benefits, especially food stamps and AFDC increases as a function of residence in concentrated poverty neighborhoods. The findings also overwhelmingly reveal that residents in concentrated poverty neighborhoods are more likely to report higher levels of criminal activity and dissatisfaction with neighborhood services—across racial and income categories.

The results present a mixed assessment of the impact of residence in concentrated poverty neighborhoods on the social networks and institutional involvement of residents. Interestingly, whites in concentrated poverty neighborhoods reported the highest levels of social isolation, but the relationships were only statistically significant among nonpoor whites. Such findings may suggest that nonpoor whites in concentrated poverty neighborhoods either make concerted efforts to separate themselves from the behavior and activity of their impoverished neighbors, or that the lack of concurrence in economic status imposes an alienating influence on nonpoor residents in concentrated poverty neighborhoods which limits their involvement in social and religious organizations. This is especially important as many social, religious and economic organizations conform to neighborhood and geographical boundaries (Huckfeldt 1986).

Substantively important differences in the viability of upwardly mobile neighborhood residents were evident among poor blacks, poor whites and nonpoor blacks, but the relationship fell just short of statistical significance at the 95% confidence level. Residence in concentrated poverty neighborhoods is also associated with limited involvement in viable institutions and organizations. However, the findings suggest that the problem of institutional viability does not permeate all concentrated poverty neighborhoods. Instead, it is most evident among poor and nonpoor whites in concentrated poverty neighborhoods, while poor and nonpoor blacks report institutional involvement, especially religious activity, regardless of income or neighborhood context. This finding is understandable, especially in light of the efforts of the South Linden community to provide outreach programs for its residents. Also, despite the decreased involvement of the black church over the last decade as noted by South Linden commissioners, it apparently still serves as a mechanism for social involvement in the black community, where similar institutions may be lacking in the predominantly white concentrated poverty neighborhood of Franklinton.

Despite the minor racial differences discussed above, the findings of this chapter are important in demonstrating that the pervasive and detrimental impact of concentrated poverty neighborhoods transcends color and class boundaries in socially isolating residents from mainstream society. The next chapter examines whether or not residence in concentrated poverty neighborhoods affects the political behavior of whites and blacks.

NOTE

1. The scale collapses the responses for satisfied and very   satisfied as well as the responses for dissatisfied and very dissatisfied.

CHAPTER 6

Neighborhood Poverty and Political Participation

INTRODUCTION

A central feature of structuralist theories of urban poverty is the assertion that there is a palpable and qualitative distinction between poor/working-class neighborhoods and concentrated poverty neighborhoods. Sociological research has verified these differences, but political scientists have lagged behind in their efforts to assess the political consequences of concentrated poverty neighborhoods. Instead, most analyses of neighborhood contexts focus primarily on working-class in contrast to middle-class neighborhoods. In fact, only two studies have attempted to examine the political consequences of concentrated neighborhood poverty. The first assessed differences between residents who lived in neighborhoods where 20% of the residents were poor as compared with neighborhoods where 10% of the residents were poor (Berry, Portney, and Thomson 1991). The findings revealed very little political difference in orientations and participation between residents in the two neighborhoods. While the study did not include neighborhoods with concentrated poverty levels, it did include a bi-racial sample which afforded an opportunity to assess racial differences in the political consequences of neighborhood poverty.

The second study focused specifically on three different types of neighborhoods, including middle-class, working-class and extremely poor neighborhoods, where at least 30% of the residents fell below the poverty line (Cohen and Dawson 1993). In contrast to the previous study, the findings revealed significant differences in the political orientations and participation rates of residents, especially between residents in neighborhoods of middle-class and high poverty neighborhoods. Differences were especially apparent in political discussion, community meetings and political communication, once the level of poverty crossed the threshold of 21%.

While both studies provided important information on the effects of neighborhood poverty, this chapter examines some of the unexplored terrain in the literature by examining the extent to which neighborhood context influences participation in electoral activities, political communication and psychological engagement in politics.

POLITICAL PARTICIPATION AND NEIGHBORHOOD CONTEXT

As a democracy, the American political system is designed with the intention that every citizen should have an equal opportunity to impact the policy process. Toward that end, both electoral and non-electoral activities were devised as a means for citizens to relay their political preferences to policy-makers. Most frequently, political scientists focus on electoral behavior including registering and voting, but more recent studies have also included campaign contributions and assistance to electoral campaigns. Far less attention has been devoted to community activity and other forms of non-electoral participation aimed at affecting political change. Such activities include attending community meetings, working with residents to solve community problems, contacting political officials, participating in demonstrations or protest marches and signing petitions in support of an issue or candidate. Both types of political activity are important in effecting change, even though voting represents the most common and inexpensive means of affecting the policy-making process.

Undergirded by structural theories of urban poverty, the analysis tests the proposition that the social context of concentrated poverty neighborhoods has a negative influence on political behavior. The spatial or geographical isolation of the neighborhoods and the concentration of poor individuals make it both costly and difficult to participate in electoral and non-electoral activities. Moreover, the debilitating condition of concentrated poverty neighborhoods possibly serves as a constant reminder of the ineffectiveness of elected officials, while the number of disenfranchised residents makes it difficult to mobilize individuals to take part in the non-electoral political activities.

Political Orientations and Neighborhood Context

Political participation studies have also demonstrated the importance of various kinds of political orientations in predicting political behavior. Some studies have focused on partisan attachment and convincingly shown that individuals with higher levels of partisan affinity are more likely to participate than those who identify as independents (Campbell, et al. 1960; Verba and Nie 1972). Other studies have shown that psychological engagement improves the likelihood of participating, whereby individuals who express interest in politics are more likely to participate than those who report that politics is not interesting to them (Campbell et al. 1954; Campbell et al. 1960; Abramson 1983; Aberbach 1969). Efficacy, which is defined as the belief that citizens can have an impact on the behavior of politicians, also has an empirical relationship to political participation. That is, individuals who believe that politicians are interested in their concerns and that they can influence the policy-making process are more likely to participate as a way of articulating their interests and desires to policy-makers (Verba and Nie 1972; Tate 1993). Finally, opinions about the effectiveness of civil disobedience have important consequences for political participation (Barnes et al. 1979). Most frequently, individuals who support the use of civil disobedience tactics including sit-ins and riots probably feel less certain about their ability to affect government decision-making through more formal electoral routes (Aberbach 1969).

Not only are the foregoing attitudes important for political participation, but they are also believed to be affected by the social context of concentrated poverty neighborhoods. In comparison to residents of low poverty neighborhoods, residents of concentrated poverty neighborhoods are expected to report lower levels of employment, educational attainment and civic engagement. Moreover, the overwhelming concern about subsistence and feelings of relative deprivation are likely to engender feelings of political abandonment and isolation which translate into low levels of political interest and efficacy, high levels of independence from political party affiliation as well as the approval of civil disobedience activities in lieu of traditional political activities.

Political Communication and Neighborhood Context

Political behavior research has demonstrated that communication among individuals has important consequences for participation in a wide array of political activities, but especially in election campaigns (Huckfeldt and Sprague 1995). According to researchers, the primary mechanism through which political communication affects political behavior is conscious and unconscious social interaction which occurs in work, church, family and neighborhood environments. Undergirded by urban poverty research and the findings of Chapter Five, this study tests the effects of neighborhood context on the political communication of residents. The hypothesis flowing from the urban poverty literature suggests that social networks are important in linking individuals to political stimuli. In contrast to individuals in working-class and middle-class neighborhoods, residents in concentrated poverty neighborhoods are expected to report fewer discussion partners with whom they discuss political issues. Also, the social context of concentrated poverty neighborhoods is expected to diminish the viability of their social networks as discussants fail to provide the necessary stimuli for political participation. Distilled from the aforementioned review of important concepts, Table 6.1 lists the three areas of political behavior that are the focus in Chapter Six.

ELECTORAL PARTICIPATION

Contrary to expectations, the findings demonstrate similar levels of electoral registration and presidential voting among whites across income levels and neighborhood context. Approximately 70% of all whites reported registering and voting in presidential elections. Also, among poor whites there are no large differences in voting in local elections, although poor whites in concentrated poverty neighborhoods reported voting slightly less than their counterparts in low poverty neighborhoods. In contrast, there is a larger gap between frequent and infrequent voters among nonpoor whites in concentrated poverty and low poverty neighborhoods, with whites in low poverty neighborhoods more likely to report frequent participation in local elections than their counterparts in concentrated poverty neighborhoods. Among nonpoor whites, participation in non-electoral activity is similar in frequency to the non-electoral activity of poor whites. Approximately 70% of nonpoor whites indicated that they had never worked with others to

Table 6.1

Concepts and Operationalizations

Concepts	Operationalizations
Political Participation	The following activities are assessed: electoral registration, voting in local elections, voting in national elections, working to solve community problems, contacting political officials, signing petitions, attending community meetings, participating in protest marches, discussing national politics, discussing local politics.
Political Orientation	Included under the umbrella of political orientation are interest in national politics, interest in local politics, political efficacy, approval of civil disobedience tactics.
Political Communication	Indicators of political communication include the following: political involvement of friends, discussion of politics with (a) family members, (b) church members, (c) coworkers, and (d) neighbors.

solve community problems or contacted a political official in the last four years. Over 80% of nonpoor whites revealed that they had not attended community meetings in the last four years.

A majority of poor blacks—regardless of differences in neighborhood context—are registered to vote. However, there are significant differences in the electoral activities of blacks in concentrated poverty and low poverty neighborhoods. Blacks in low poverty neighborhoods are considerably more likely to report that they voted in presidential and local elections than their counterparts in concentrated poverty neighborhoods.

Statistically significant differences are evident in electoral activities of nonpoor blacks across neighborhood social contexts. Among nonpoor blacks, a slightly higher percentage of residents in low poverty neighborhoods are registered to vote. Also, nonpoor blacks in low poverty neighborhoods are more likely to report that they voted in presidential elections than their counterparts in low poverty neighborhoods. The differences in local electoral activity of nonpoor blacks are substantively small and statistically insignificant.

In a large measure, Table 6.2 provides only partial support for the contention that concentrated poverty neighborhoods depress electoral activity. The findings demonstrated that the electoral activities of

Table 6.2
Electoral Activities in Concentrated Poverty and Low Poverty Neighborhoods

Responses	Poor Whites		Nonpoor Whites		Poor Blacks		Nonpoor Blacks	
	Concentrated Poverty	Low Poverty	Concentrated Poverty	Low Poverty	Concentrated Poverty	Low Poverty	Concentrated Poverty	Low Poverty
Registered to vote								
Yes	68	65	71	76	85	94	88*	94
No	32	35	29	24	15	6	12	6
Voted in presidential elections								
Hardly ever	31	23	30	25	22*	6	15*	9
Most of the time	69	77	70	75	78	94	85	91
Voted in local elections								
Hardly ever	42	33	39**	30	22**	7	16	13
Most of the time	58	67	61	70	78	93	84	87

Source: 1991 Columbus Neighborhood Study Data Set.
***$p \leq .001$; **$p \leq .01$; *$p \leq .05$.

whites are less influenced by residence in concentrated poverty neighborhoods than blacks. Additionally, the findings suggest that the electoral activities of poor blacks are diminished to a much greater extent by residence in concentrated poverty neighborhoods than their nonpoor counterparts.

NONELECTORAL PARTICIPATION

The analysis of nonelectoral findings (Table 6.3) reveals limited participation in such activities. Approximately 80% of poor whites in concentrated poverty and low poverty neighborhoods indicated that they had never worked with others to solve community problems or signed petitions. Over 85% of poor whites in concentrated poverty and low poverty neighborhoods reported that they had never attended a community meeting in the last four years. Approximately 55% of poor whites in concentrated poverty and low poverty neighborhoods, regardless of neighborhood context reported that they do not discuss either local or national politics often. Significant differences among poor whites were only noted in the area of contacting political officials. Compared with 15% of poor whites in low poverty neighborhoods, 32% of poor whites in concentrated poverty neighborhoods reported contacting political officials in the last four years. Since concentrated poverty residents are more likely to be beleaguered by less efficient neighborhood services (Chapter 5), it is not surprising that they are more likely to contact political officials in an effort to remedy the problems.

Significant differences in non-electoral activity as a result of neighborhood contexts were evident in the frequency of political discussions as well as the extent to which individuals participated in signing petitions in support of candidates or issues and contacting political officials. Compared with nonpoor whites in concentrated neighborhoods, their counterparts in low poverty neighborhoods were much more likely to report that they frequently discuss national politics. They are also more likely to contact political officials than their counterparts in low poverty neighborhoods. In contrast, nonpoor whites in low poverty neighborhoods were more likely than their counterparts in concentrated poverty neighborhoods to report that they had signed petitions for candidates or issues in the last four years.

As illustrated in Table 6.4, few differences are evident in the non-electoral activities of poor blacks in concentrated poverty and low

Table 6.3: Non-Electoral Activity among Whites in Concentrated Poverty and Low Poverty Neighborhoods

	Poor Whites		Non-Poor Whites	
Responses	Concentrated Poverty	Low Poverty	Concentrated Poverty	Low Poverty
Worked to solve community problems				
Never	76	85	70	67
Once/more than once	24	15	30	33
N	133	133	482	482
Contacted political officials				
Never	68*	85	63*	72
Once/more than once	32	15	37	28
N	133	133	480	480
Signed petitions for candidates				
Never	66	59	57*	48
Once/more than once	34	41	43	52
N	131	131	479	479
Attended community meetings				
Never	86	89	82	78
Once/more than once	14	11	18	22
N	129	129	475	475
Discussed local politics				
Never	60	67	50*	59
Once/more than once	40	33	50	41
N	132	132	481	481
Discussed national politics				
Never	49	52	64*	74
Once/more than once	51	48	36	26
N	132	132	480	480

Source: 1991 Columbus Neighborhood Study Data Set.

*** $p \leq .001$; ** $p \leq .01$; * $p \leq .05$.

poverty neighborhoods. Almost 70% of poor blacks reported that they never worked to solve community problems, or signed petitions in support of issues or candidates. Of poor blacks, 85% reported that they never contacted political officials, while approximately 50% indicated that they do not frequently discuss either local or national politics.

Significant differences were evident across predominantly black neighborhood contexts, however, in attending community meetings. Poor blacks in concentrated poverty were more likely to report that they attended community meetings than their counterparts. This finding contrasts with the expectation that concentrated poverty neighborhoods depress community activities. Instead, it suggests that neighborhood residents are more likely to mobilize themselves in such activity because there is more of a need in concentrated poverty neighborhoods than in others. These findings are consistent with a prior study which demonstrated how neighborhood residents mobilized themselves to participate in non-electoral activities in spite of the environmental constraints of the neighborhood (Crenson 1983).

Regardless of neighborhood social context, a majority of nonpoor blacks reported that they never worked to solve problems, contact political officials or sign petitions in support of an issue or candidate. However, significant neighborhood differences were evident among blacks who attended community meetings and protest marches. Nonpoor blacks in concentrated poverty neighborhoods were more likely to attend community meetings but less likely to participate in protest marches and demonstrations. Although nonpoor blacks, regardless of neighborhood context, frequently discuss local politics, nonpoor blacks in concentrated poverty neighborhoods are less likely than their counterparts in low poverty neighborhoods to discuss national politics.

Overall, the findings shown in Tables 6.3–6.4 do not support the contention that concentrated poverty neighborhoods depress non-electoral activity. Instead, the findings unequivocally demonstrate that participation in non-electoral activities among whites and blacks in concentrated poverty neighborhoods generally exceeds that of residents in low poverty neighborhoods. Such findings mirror the results of two earlier studies which demonstrated hyperactivity among poor residents in economically depressed neighborhoods (Crenson 1983; Berry, Portney and Thomson 1993).

Table 6.4: Non-Electoral Activity among Blacks in Concentrated Poverty and Low Poverty Neighborhoods

Responses	Poor Blacks		Nonpoor Blacks	
	Concentrated Poverty	Low Poverty	Concentrated Poverty	Low Poverty
Worked to solve community problems				
Never	66	76	63	56
Once/more than once	34	24	37	44
N	178	178	492	492
Contacted political officials				
Never	85	85	77	70
Once/more than once	15	15	23	30
N	178	178	487	487
Signed petitions for candidates				
Never	60	69	49	47
Once/more than once	40	31	41	53
N	174	174	493	493
Attended community meetings				
Never	74*	90	68*	77
Once/more than once	26	10	32	23
N	177	177	490	490
Discussed local politics				
Never	49	47	35	32
Once/more than once	51	53	65	68
N	176	176	491	491
Discussed national politics				
Never	48	50	35*	28
Once/more than once	52	50	65	72
N	176	176	490	490

Source: 1991 Columbus Neighborhood Study Data Set.

*** $p \leq .001$; ** $p \leq .01$; * $p \leq .05$.

POLITICAL ORIENTATIONS

Tables 6.5 and 6.6 present the results for political orientations. Among poor whites there is little differentiation in political orientations across neighborhood social contexts. Over 60% of the poor reported that they were interested or very interested in politics, while over 50% disagreed with the idea that the public has control over politicians. Moreover, there is little of the expected differentiation along partisan lines. There are slightly more independents in concentrated poverty neighborhoods, but the difference is not large enough to boast of statistical or substantive importance. Also, the majority of poor whites, regardless of neighborhood context, disapprove of rioting. In fact, the only substantively and statistically important difference between poor whites in concentrated poverty and low poverty neighborhood is their attitude about sit-ins and demonstrations. Poor whites in concentrated poverty neighborhoods are twice as likely as their counterparts in low poverty neighborhoods to approve of using sit-ins to stop government, even though a majority of poor whites disagreed with the tactic. This finding provides support for the contention that residents in concentrated poverty neighborhoods are more likely to utilize political activities that are outside the electoral realm than their counterparts in low poverty neighborhoods.

The effect of neighborhood context on the political orientations of nonpoor whites is mixed. An overwhelming majority of nonpoor whites report interest in national politics. In keeping with expectations, nonpoor whites in concentrated poverty neighborhoods were more likely to identify as independents than their counterparts in low poverty neighborhoods. However, nonpoor whites in both concentrated poverty and low poverty neighborhoods express similar levels of limited faith in the idea that the public has control over politicians. Also, nonpoor whites in both poor and nonpoor neighborhoods are at par in their support of sit-ins and demonstrations to stop government. However, nonpoor whites in concentrated poverty neighborhoods are more likely than nonpoor whites in low poverty neighborhoods to approve of rioting.

Few differences emerge among the sampled political orientations of poor blacks, as shown in Table 6.6. A majority of poor blacks, regardless of neighborhood residence, reported little interest in national politics. Over 70% of poor blacks identified themselves as Democrats. Moreover, there are very low levels of political efficacy among poor

Table 6.5: Political Orientations among Whites in Concentrated Poverty and Low Poverty Neighborhoods

	Poor Whites		Nonpoor Whites	
Responses	Concentrated Poverty	Low Poverty	Concentrated Poverty	Low Poverty
Interest in national politics				
Yes	62	59	88	81
No	28	41	22	19
N	132	132	479	479
Have a partisan preference				
Republicans	26	35	25**	34
Democrats	34	39	32	36
Independents	36	15	41	24
Others	4	11	2	6
N	126	126	457	457
Believe in public control over politicians				
Yes	46	43	35	31
No	54	57	65	69
N	115	115	449	449
Approve of stopping government with sit-ins and demonstrations				
Yes	45**	21	52	55
No	55	79	48	45
N	119	119	439	439
Approve of stopping government by rioting				
Yes	24	16	20**	10
No	76	84	80	98
N	123	123	455	455

Source: 1991 Columbus Neighborhood Study Data Set.

*** $p \leq .001$; ** $p \leq .01$; * $p \leq .05$.

Table 6.6: Political Orientations among Blacks in Concentrated Poverty and Low Poverty Neighborhoods

	Poor Blacks		Nonpoor Blacks	
Responses	Concentrated Poverty	Low Poverty	Concentrated Poverty	Low Poverty
Interest in national politics				
Yes	26	20	19*	12
No	74	80	81	88
N	173	173	488	488
Have a partisan preference				
Republicans	7	6	4	3
Democrats	72	79	76	80
Independents	19	12	17	16
Others	2	3	3	1
N	168	168	473	473
Believe in public control over politicians				
Yes	41	43	38	35
No	59	57	62	65
N	164	164	467	467
Approve of stopping government with sit-ins and demonstrations				
Yes	46*	25	62	65
No	54	75	38	35
N	149	149	436	436
Approve of stopping government by rioting				
Yes	28	36	28	31
No	72	64	72	69
N	156	156	446	446

Source: 1991 Columbus Neighborhood Study Data Set.

*** $p \leq .001$; ** $p \leq .01$; * $p \leq .05$.

blacks in both neighborhoods as a majority agreed with the statement that the public has no control over politicians. Similar to their white counterparts, a majority of poor blacks in concentrated poverty and low poverty neighborhoods disapprove of rioting. However, substantively and statistically important differences emerge on orientations toward sit-ins and demonstrations. Poor blacks in concentrated poverty neighborhoods are almost twice as likely to approve of protests and demonstrations than their counterparts in low poverty neighborhoods.

As the results of Table 6.6 demonstrate, nonpoor blacks do not express different kinds of political orientations across neighborhood contexts. A majority of nonpoor blacks report loyalty to the Democratic party, as well as low levels of political efficacy. Nonpoor blacks are also more likely to approve of government sit-ins and demonstrations than of rioting, however there are no differences across neighborhood social contexts. In fact, the only substantive and statistical differences occur with respect to interest in national politics. Nonpoor blacks in concentrated poverty neighborhoods were somewhat more interested in national politics than their counterparts in low poverty neighborhoods.

POLITICAL COMMUNICATION

Tables 6.7 and 6.8 delineate the findings for political communication among whites and blacks, respectively. Contrary to expectations, the findings do not reveal significant differences in the political communication of poor whites across neighborhood social contexts. A majority of poor whites, regardless of neighborhood context, reported that the people they know are interested in local and national politics. The analysis also revealed that neighborhood context is not related to political discussions with family members or co-workers. However, differences were evident with respect to church and neighborhood environments. Poor whites in concentrated poverty neighborhoods are three times more likely to report that they discuss politics with someone at church than their counterparts in low poverty neighborhoods. Also, compared to 57% of poor whites in concentrated poverty neighborhoods, 38% of poor whites in low poverty neighborhoods reported talking to neighbors about politics. Contrary to expectations, these findings indicated that among poor whites, impoverished neighborhood context does not stifle political discussion. This is

Table 6.7: Political Communication among Whites in Concentrated Poverty and Low Poverty Neighborhoods

Responses	Poor Whites		Nonpoor Whites	
	Concentrated Poverty	Low Poverty	Concentrated Poverty	Low Poverty
People you know interested in national politics				
Interested	64	79	63**	77
Not interested	36	21	37	23
N	109	109	447	447
People you know interested in local politics				
Interested	80	74	81*	88
Not interested	20	26	19	12
N	108	108	444	444
Discuss politics with family members				
Yes	72	76	80	85
No	28	24	20	15
N	104	104	423	423
Discuss politics with someone at church				
Yes	28*	9	29	30
No	72	91	71	70
N	104	104	422	422
Discuss politics with someone at work				
Yes	28	27	56	63
No	72	73	46	37
N	104	104	420	420
Discuss politics with someone in neighborhood				
Yes	57	38	55	51
No	43	62	45	49
N	104	104	422	422

Source: 1991 Columbus Neighborhood Study Data Set.

*** $p \leq .001$; ** $p \leq .01$; * $p \leq .05$.

especially important because such institutions often serve as the site for political recruitment and stimuli. As a result, it is not surprising that whites and blacks in concentrated poverty neighborhoods were more likely to participate in non-electoral activities than their counterparts in low poverty neighborhoods.

Consistent with expectations, the findings demonstrate that neighborhood context affects the political discussions among nonpoor whites. Nonpoor whites in concentrated poverty neighborhoods, are less likely than their counterparts to report interest in national and local politics. This is important because such discussion partners provide a sense of political stimulus for political activity that residents in concentrated poverty neighborhoods are not afforded. Regardless of neighborhood context, however, a majority of nonpoor whites reported that they discussed politics with family members, someone at work and someone in the neighborhood, while fewer individuals reported discussing politics with fellow religious worshippers.

Contrary to expectations, residence in concentrated poverty neighborhoods does not considerably impact the political communication of poor blacks (Table 6.8). Poor blacks in concentrated poverty and low poverty neighborhoods report high levels of interest in local and national politics among people they know. Moreover, an equally high percentage of poor blacks indicate that they discuss politics with their family members and someone at church. Similar to poor and nonpoor whites, the findings indicate that work environments do not serve to facilitate discussions about politics as approximately 75% of poor blacks in both neighborhoods reveal that they do not discuss politics with co-workers. However, a substantively significant difference in discussions with neighbors indicates that poor blacks in concentrated poverty neighborhoods are significantly more likely to discuss politics with someone in the neighborhood than residents in low poverty neighborhoods. Such findings might reflect the hyperactivity that occurs among some residents in concentrated poverty neighborhoods who are resolved to participate in politics as a way of improving the condition of their neighborhoods.

The nature and depth of political discussion are similar between nonpoor blacks in concentrated poverty and low poverty neighborhoods. A majority of nonpoor blacks report that the people they know express interest in local and national politics. Regardless of neighborhood context, a majority of nonpoor blacks reported that they

Table 6.8: Political Communication among Blacks in Concentrated Poverty and Low Poverty Neighborhoods

Responses	Poor Blacks		Nonpoor Blacks	
	Concentrated Poverty	Low Poverty	Concentrated Poverty	Low Poverty
People you know interested in national politics				
Interested	78	83	83	87
Not interested	22	17	17	13
N	153	153	460	460
People you know interested in local politics				
Interested	75	79	82	88
Not interested	25	21	18	12
N	156	156	463	463
Discuss politics with family members				
Yes	80	82	83	91
No	20	18	17	9
N	154	154	454	454
Discuss politics with someone at church				
Yes	57	48	60	55
No	43	52	40	45
N	154	154	452	452
Discuss politics with someone at work				
Yes	27	18	58	65
No	73	82	42	35
N	153	153	447	447
Discuss politics with someone in neighborhood				
Yes	57*	37	58	56
No	43	63	42	44
N	155	155	454	454

Source: 1991 Columbus Neighborhood Study Data Set.

*** $p \le .001$; ** $p \le .01$; * $p \le .05$.

discussed problems with someone at church, work and in the neighborhood.

SUMMARY AND DISCUSSION

The findings of this chapter have provided interesting answers to some important, but unaddressed questions about the role of concentrated poverty neighborhoods on political behavior. Overall, the results provide mixed support for the contention that concentrated poverty neighborhoods facilitate different kinds of political activities and behaviors than working and middle-class neighborhoods. First, neighborhood contextual effects were most important with respect to political participation and least important in political communication. As predicted, blacks and whites in concentrated poverty neighborhoods were somewhat less likely to vote than their counterparts in low poverty neighborhoods. Conversely, analyses of non-electoral participation revealed that whites and blacks in concentrated poverty neighborhoods were more likely to participate in some non-electoral activities than their counterparts. For example, whites in concentrated poverty neighborhoods were more likely to report that they contacted political officials than their counterparts in low poverty neighborhoods. Poor blacks in concentrated poverty neighborhoods were more likely to attend community meetings.

Although these findings are contrary to the urban poverty thesis, they are explainable. Concentrated poverty neighborhoods have higher levels of neighborhood dissatisfaction and problems, as revealed by the findings in Chapter Five. It is not surprising then, that residents of these neighborhoods would make more contact with officials or attend community meetings in an effort to redress these problems.

Meanwhile, it is important to notice the difference in the activities that whites and blacks utilized in concentrated poverty neighborhoods. Whites contacted political officials, while their black counterparts attended community meetings to resolve problems. This more formalized tactic used by whites as compared with the grass-roots tactic utilized by blacks suggests that whites have greater direct access to the policy-making process than their black counterparts. It also lends credence to the contention made by Clarence Lumpkin, one of the founding members of the South Linden Neighborhood Association, as he underscored the relatively lower level of access that blacks have in the policy-making process. At a more fundamental level, the findings suggest that while whites and blacks are similarly affected by debilitating contextual factors, whites may have a wider range of ameliorative options.

Important neighborhood differences were also evident among policy orientations. Poor whites and blacks in concentrated poverty neighborhoods were more likely to approve of civil disobedience tactics as a means of affecting the policy process. These orientations are consistent with lower levels of electoral participation and higher levels of non-electoral participation as evinced in the findings for political participation. Unfortunately, these findings suggest that poor whites and blacks in concentrated poverty neighborhoods are disconnected from the formal mechanisms of participation, and many approve of civil disobedience tactics as a potent way of focusing public policy attention on their plight. While neighborhood context is important, as the findings for this chapter have revealed, family context is also important. The next chapter assesses the extent to which residence in single-parent households affects the social and political behavior of whites and blacks.

CHAPTER 7

Does Family Context Matter?

INTRODUCTION

Over the past two decades, America has generally witnessed a dramatic transformation in the structure of families. Households headed by never married, separated and divorced women with children have grown from being statistically insignificant to commonplace (McLanahan and Garfinkel 1989; McLanahan 1995; McLanahan and Sandefur 1994). Recently, single-parent households have become the political and economic scapegoats of some politicians and religious groups, receiving the blame for some aspects of America's so-called moral erosion. It is important to underscore, therefore, that this study does not address the moral ramifications of single-parent households, and its implications should not be construed as a statement on the same.

Instead, the goal of Chapter Seven is to assess the socio-economic and political consequences of family structure for whites and blacks in inner-city communities. The literature on family structure has postulated that single-parent households have a number of disadvantages, including greater psychological stress, decreased income, frequent changes in residence and employment as well as social isolation in the form of diminished social networks and support systems (McLanahan and Sandefur 1994; McLanahan 1995). Other studies have suggested that single-parent households have played a major role in creating an underclass (Wilson 1987). Reportedly, children from single-parent households are more likely to drop out of school, to be unemployed and to form mother-only families themselves (Wilson 1987).

Also, single-parent households are known to be more vulnerable to poverty and social isolation. Previous studies have documented that individuals in single-parent households are more likely to express feelings of alienation and cynicism since they are often alienated from individuals in the social and economic mainstream (Auletta 1982; Wilson and Wacquant 1989; McLanahan and Garfinkel 1989). Additionally, individuals in single-parent households are less likely to benefit from durable ties to social and religious organizations, which would often facilitate participation (Nelson 1984).

Indeed, there are multifarious burdens on single-parent households, including the cumbersome burden of single-handedly caring for the needs of children as well as being the only bread-winner. These known situations are expected to diminish the amount of attention that individuals in female-headed households can give to political activities, as the struggle for economic survival comes first and foremost (Nelson 1984).

Absent from many of the previously mentioned analyses, however, is an understanding of racial variations in the consequences of family structure, especially as they pertain to socio-economic factors and political behavior. Consequently, the first section of this chapter is devoted to an examination of the extent to which single-parent households experience higher levels of economic marginalization than two-parent households. This chapter examines important indicators of economic marginalization, including joblessness, whether or not households receive AFDC or food stamps, and the extent to which households rent and own automobiles. In keeping with the poverty research as well as the research on single-parent families, this research posits that individuals in single-parent households will experience more economic marginalization than individuals in two-parent households.

The second section of this chapter examines the relationship between family structure and a host of political behaviors including political participation, political orientations and political communication. Three additional hypotheses guide the analyses of the relationship between political behavior and family structure. First, individuals in single-parent households are less likely to participate in all kinds of political activities but especially in non-electoral activities because of the high level of time and resource commitment necessary. Second, individuals in single-parent households are expected to harbor more negative views of the political system than their counterparts in two-parent households. Third, the political communication of individuals in single-parent households is expected to be limited as compared with individuals in two-parent households. Toward that end, respondents were divided into one of eight categories: poor, single-parent whites, poor single-parent blacks, nonpoor single-parent blacks, nonpoor single-parent whites, poor two-parent whites, poor two-parent blacks, nonpoor two-parent blacks and nonpoor two-parent whites. Contingency table analysis was utilized to assess differences across the categories.

The concepts and operationalizations that will be utilized to test the foregoing hypothesis are listed in Table 7.1 below:

Table 7.1
Concepts and Operationalizations

Concepts	Operationalizations
Economic Marginalization	Measures the extent to which residents are jobless, dependent on welfare benefits and food stamps, own automobiles and homes.
Political Participation	The following activities are assessed: electoral registration, voting in local elections, voting in national elections, working to solve community problems, contacting political officials, signing petitions, attending community meetings, participating in protest marches, discussing national politics, discussing local politics.
Political Orientations	Included under the umbrella of political orientations are interest in national politics, interest in local politics, sense of political efficacy, approval of civil disobedience tactics.
Political Communication	Indicators of political communication include the following: political involvement of friends, discussion of politics with (a) family members, (b) church members, (c) coworkers, and (d) neighbors.

ECONOMIC MARGINALIZATION AND FAMILY STRUCTURE

As demonstrated by the findings illustrated in Figures 7.1, 7.2, 7.3 and 7.4, family context is statistically associated with economic marginalization. Poor whites in single-parent households are almost twice as likely to be unemployed as compared with their counterparts in

Figure 7.1:
Economic Marginalization among Poor Inner-City Whites: A Comparison of
Single-Parent and Two-Parent Households

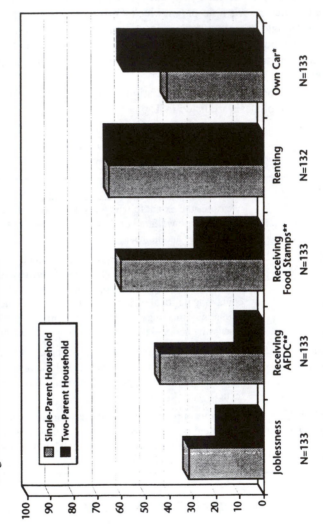

Source: 1991 Columbus Neighborhood Study Data Set.

*** $p \leq .001$; ** $p \leq .01$; * $p \leq .05$.

Figure 7.2:
Economic Marginalization among Non-poor Inner-City Whites: A Comparison of Single-Parent and Two-Parent Households

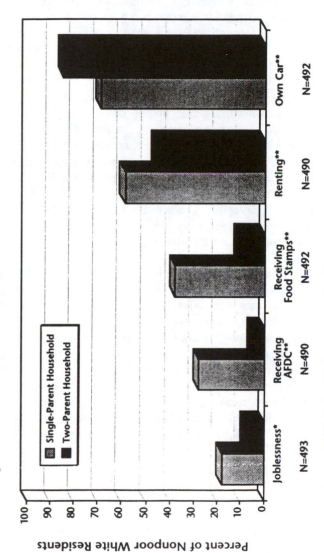

Source: 1991 Columbus Neighborhood Study Data Set.

*** $p \leq .001$; ** $p \leq .01$; * $p \leq .05$.

two-parent households. Over 40% of poor whites in single-parent households receive AFDC, compared with only 10% in two-parent households. The percentage of poor whites who received food stamps in single-parent households is more than double that of poor whites in two-parent households. While the percentage of poor whites in two-parent households who rent homes is at par with their counterparts in single-parent households, there are substantively and statistically important differences in automobile ownership. Poor whites in two-parent households are much more likely to own an automobile than their counterparts in single-parent households.

The degree of economic marginalization is even more alarming among nonpoor whites in single-parent households. Compared to their counterparts in two-parent households, nonpoor whites in single-parent family structures are over twice as likely to report being jobless, almost six times more likely to report that they receive AFDC, and three times more likely to report that they receive food stamps. Differences are also evident in home and car ownership, where 13% and 16% gaps exist between the ownership rates of nonpoor whites in single-parent and two-parent households.

The pattern of economic marginalization that existed among poor single-parent whites is similar among poor blacks. While there is little substantive or statistical difference in the joblessness rate of poor blacks in single-parent and two-parent households, there are large and statistically significant differences in the percentage of AFDC and food stamp recipients as well as car and home ownership. Almost three times as many poor blacks in single-parent households receive AFDC and food stamp benefits as compared with poor blacks in two-parent households. The percentage of poor blacks in single-parent households who rent is double that of poor blacks in two-parent households. Car ownership is considerably more prevalent among poor blacks in two-parent households as compared with their counterparts in single-parent households.

Among nonpoor blacks in single-parent households, economic marginalization is also a reality. Nonpoor blacks in single-parent households are three times more likely to receive AFDC and food stamp benefits. The percentage of nonpoor blacks in single-parent households who rent is almost twice the rate of nonpoor blacks in two-parent households. The economic marginalization among nonpoor blacks is not as severe among poor blacks. For example, a relatively low rate of joblessness exists among nonpoor blacks in either single-

Figure 7.3:
Economic Marginalization among Poor Inner-City Blacks: A Comparison of Single-Parent and Two-Parent Households

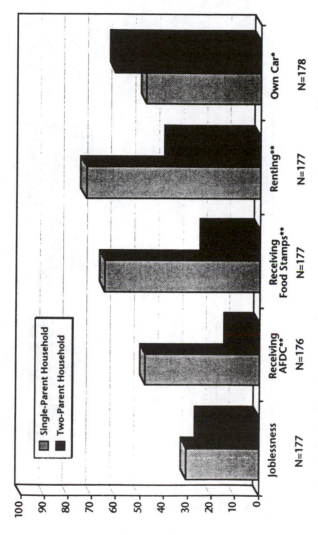

Source: 1991 Columbus Neighborhood Study Data Set.

*** $p \leq .001$; ** $p \leq .01$; * $p \leq .05$.

Figure 7.4:
Economic Marginalization among Non-poor Inner-City Blacks: A Comparison of Single-Parent and Two-Parent Households

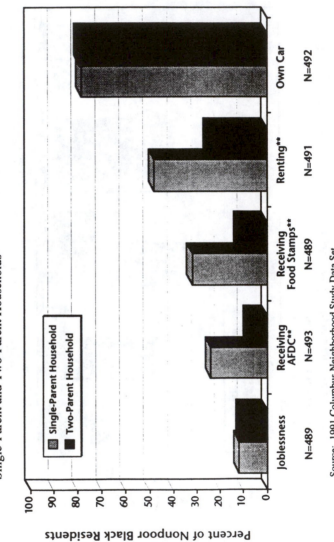

Source: 1991 Columbus Neighborhood Study Data Set.

*** $p \leq .001$; ** $p \leq .01$; * $p \leq .05$.

parent or two-parent households. There is also a high rate of car ownership among nonpoor blacks, regardless of family structure.

As compared with their counterparts in two-parent households, poor and nonpoor blacks and whites in single-parent family structures experience higher levels of economic marginalization in terms of joblessness, dependence on government benefits, and the lack of car and home ownership. It is posited that economic marginalization of single-parent household structures has important political consequences. The second part of this chapter assesses the validity of this claim.

ELECTORAL ACTIVITY AND FAMILY STRUCTURE

Table 7.2 delineates the findings of cross-table analysis for poor whites, nonpoor whites, poor blacks and nonpoor blacks. Consistent with expectations, there are substantively and statistically important differences in the electoral participation of poor whites in single-parent and two-parent households. Less than 50% of poor whites in single-parent households reported that they were registered to vote, compared with 74% of poor whites in two-parent household structures. Similar differences are evident with respect to voting in presidential elections. Compared with 56% of poor whites in single-parent households, almost 75% of poor whites in two-parent households report voting in presidential elections most of the time. In local elections 50% of individuals in single-parent households reported voting compared with 64% in two-parent households.

Among nonpoor whites, statistically significant differences are evident in registering and participating in presidential elections. Compared with 59% of nonpoor whites in single-parent households, 76% of nonpoor whites in two-parent households reported that they were registered to vote. Additionally, among single-parent households, about 40% reported that they hardly ever voted in presidential elections. Differences in local electoral participation were small and statistically insignificant.

Among poor blacks, there are substantively and statistically significant differences in local and presidential electoral activities. Blacks in single-parent households are about three times as likely as blacks in two-parent households to report that they hardly ever vote in presidential and local elections.

Table 7.2
Family Structure and Electoral Activity

Responses	Poor Whites		Nonpoor Whites		Poor Blacks		Nonpoor Blacks	
	One-Parent	Two-Parent	One-Parent	Two-Parent	One-Parent	Two-Parent	One-Parent	Two-Parent
Registered to vote								
Yes	49**	74	59**	76	85	88	88	91
No	51	26	41	23	15	12	12	8
N	131	131	477	477	177	177	492	492
Voted in presidential elections								
Hardly ever	44*	24	38*	25	21*	6	15*	9
Most of the time	56	75	62	75	79	94	85	91
N	131	131	480	480	177	177	491	491
Voted in local elections								
Hardly ever	50	36	41	34	22*	7	16	13
Most of the time	50	64	59	66	78	93	84	87
N	133	133	480	480	177	177	491	491

Source: 1991 Columbus Neighborhood Study Data Set.
***$p \leq .001$; **$p \leq .01$; *$p \leq .05$.

A contrasting set of findings exist for nonpoor blacks. Nonpoor blacks—in both single-parent and two-parent households—also overwhelmingly reported that they voted most of the time in presidential and local elections. The only statistically salient difference across family context occurred with respect to voting in presidential elections, but the substantive differences are not very large.

NON-ELECTORAL ACTIVITY AND FAMILY STRUCTURE

Contingency table analysis results for poor and nonpoor whites are presented in Table 7.3. Differences in the non-electoral participation of poor whites in single-parent and two-parent households are much smaller than the differences in electoral activity; few activities are differentiated by family structure. Between 60% and 80% of poor whites, regardless of family structure, indicated that they never worked with others to solve community problems, contacted political officials or signed petitions in support of candidates or issues. However, poor whites in single-parent households are somewhat less likely to attend community meetings than their counterparts in two-parent households. Important substantive differences were evident in the frequency with which poor whites in single-parent and two-parent households discussed politics. Contrary to expectations, poor whites in single-parent households were more likely than their counterparts in two-parent households to report that they discussed politics. Perhaps this frequency in political discussion was a result of the recent harsh economic and social policies that have negatively impacted single-parent households over the last two decades. The differences were larger for discussions of local politics as compared with national politics.

Among nonpoor whites, there are very few differences in non-electoral activities in single-parent versus two-parent households. Nonpoor whites were largely inactive in non-electoral activities. Over 60% of nonpoor whites, regardless of family structure, reported that they never worked to solve community problems, contacted political officials or attended community meetings. A majority of nonpoor whites (over 50%) also reported a lack of interest in signing petitions in support of issues or candidates. Differences were evident, however, in regard to discussions of local and national politics. As compared with their counterparts in single-parent households, nonpoor whites in two-

Table 7.3: Family Structure and Non-Electoral Activity among Whites

Responses	Poor Whites		Nonpoor Whites	
	One-Parent	Two-Parent	One-Parent	Two-Parent
Worked to solve community problems				
Never	82	76	64	70
Once or more	18	24	36	30
N	133	133	482	482
Contacted political officials				
Never	68	73	66	67
Once or more	32	27	34	33
N	133	133	480	480
Signed petitions for candidates				
Never	71	63	56	53
Once or more	29	37	44	47
N	131	131	479	479
Attended community meetings				
Never	94	84	79	81
Once or more	6	16	21	19
N	129	129	475	475
Discussed local politics				
Not too often/somewhat	29*	43	56*	44
Very often/often	71	57	44	56
N	132	132	481	481
Discussed national politics				
Not too often/somewhat	44**	53	45*	30
Very often/often	56	47	55	70
N	132	132	480	480

Source: 1991 Colur . s Neighborhood Study Data Set.

*** $p \leq .001$; ** $p \leq$.;; * $p \leq .05$.

Table 7.4: Family Structure and Non-Electoral Activity among Blacks

	Poor Blacks		Nonpoor Blacks	
Responses	One-Parent	Two-Parent	One-Parent	Two-Parent
Worked to solve community problems				
Never	66	69	64	70
Once or more	18	24	36	30
N	133	133	482	482
Contacted political officials				
Never	68	73	66	67
Once or more	32	27	34	33
N	133	133	480	480
Signed petitions for candidates				
Never	71	63	56	53
Once or more	29	37	44	47
N	131	131	479	479
Attended community meetings				
Never	94	84	79	81
Once or more	6	16	21	19
N	129	129	475	475
Discussed local politics				
Not too often/somewhat	29*	43	56*	44
Very often/often	71	57	44	56
N	132	132	481	481
Discussed national politics				
Not too often/somewhat	44**	53	45*	30
Very often/often	56	47	55	70
N	132	132	480	480

Source: 1991 Columbus Neighborhood Study Data Set.

*** $p \leq .001$; ** $p \leq .01$; * $p \leq .05$.

parent households were much more likely to report that they frequently discussed local and national politics.

Most poor blacks in both single-parent and two-parent households are uninvolved in non-electoral activities. Almost 70% never worked to solve community problems, and approximately 80% never contacted political officials or attended community meetings. Furthermore, over 50% of poor blacks reported that they infrequently discuss local and national politics. Poor blacks in single-parent households are more likely than their counterparts to report that they signed petitions, a substantively important but statistically insignificant finding. Among poor blacks, family structure had little impact on non-electoral activity.

Contrary to expectations, there are no substantive or statistically salient differences in the non-electoral participation of nonpoor blacks in single-parent and two-parent households. Approximately 60% of nonpoor blacks, regardless of differences in family structure, reported that they never worked to solve community problems and that they discussed local and national politics infrequently. Over 70% of nonpoor blacks in both single-parent and two-parent households stated that they never contacted political officials or attended community meetings.

POLITICAL ORIENTATIONS AND FAMILY STRUCTURE

The findings for political orientations among poor and nonpoor whites are presented in Table 7.5. Some political orientations among poor whites were affected by family structure, while others were not. For example, regardless of differences in family structure, poor whites overwhelmingly reported a lack of interest in national politics. However, substantive and statistically important differences were evident with respect to partisan affiliation, efficacy (belief in public control over political officials) and approval of civil disobedience tactics. Poor whites in single-parent households were much more likely than their counterparts in two-parent households to identify themselves as political independents. Also, compared with almost 50% of poor whites in two-parent households, approximately 70% of poor whites in single-parent households disagreed with the notion that the public has control over politicians. While most poor whites, regardless of differences in family structure, disapproved of rioting, poor whites in single-parent households were significantly more likely to approve of engaging in sit-ins and demonstrations as a way of influencing the governmental process.

Table 7.5: Family Structure and Political Oreintations among Poor and Nonpoor Whites

| | Poor Whites | | Nonpoor Whites | |
Responses	One-Parent	Two-Parent	One-Parent	Two-Parent
Interest in national politics				
Interested	35	29	27	20
Not too interested	65	71	73	80
N	132	132	479	479
Have a partisan preference				
Republicans	22***	30	18***	30
Democrats	16	42	23	36
Independents	6	5	10	3
Others	126	126	467	467
N				
Believe in public control over politicians				
Yes	32*	49	34	33
No	68	51	66	67
N	115	115	449	449
Stop government with sit-ins and demonstrations				
Yes	54*	36	54	53
No	46	64	46	47
N	119	119	439	439
Stop government by rioting				
Yes	14	25	13	17
No	86	75	87	83
N	123	123	455	455

Source: 1991 Columbus Neighborhood Study Data Set.

*** $p \le .001$; ** $p \le .01$; * $p \le .05$.

In a large measure, nonpoor whites expressed similar political attitudes regardless of differences in family structure. Nonpoor whites in both single-parent and two-parent households overwhelmingly reported a lack of interest in national and local politics as well as a lack of political efficacy. Nonpoor whites in both single-parent and two-parent households also expressed similar levels of disapproval for demonstrations and sit-ins. However, differences across family contexts emerged in partisan preferences. Nonpoor whites in single-parent households are less loyal to political parties than their counterparts in two-parent households, who are most likely to identify as Democrats.

Differences across family context are also evident among blacks as the findings in Table 7.6 reveal. Indeed, poor blacks in single-parent and two-parent households report similar levels of political efficacy and approval for civil disobedience tactics. However, poor blacks in two-parent and single-parent households report different levels of interest in national politics as well as partisan identification. In contrast to the expectation that residence in single-parent households reduces political interest, the findings suggest that poor blacks in single-parent households were more likely to report higher levels of interest in national politics. This interest in politics may be the result of the increasingly harsh and combative political environment that scapegoats mother-only families, especially black single-parent households as the root of America's economic and social problems. Consistent with expectations, however, is the finding that poor blacks in single-parent households are less loyal to the Democratic Party and much more likely to identify as political independents.

There are no important differences between the political orientations of nonpoor blacks in single-parent and two-parent households. Regardless of family structure, nonpoor blacks report low levels of interest in national politics, low levels of political efficacy, overwhelming approval of sit-ins and demonstrations and overwhelming disapproval of rioting. A majority of nonpoor blacks in single-parent and two-parent households identify as Democrats.

POLITICAL COMMUNICATION AND FAMILY STRUCTURE

Family context is not only expected to influence economic well-being, political participation and political orientations, it is also expected to

Table 7.6: Family Structure and Political Oreintations among Poor and Nonpoor Blacks

Responses	Poor Blacks		Nonpoor Blacks	
	One-Parent	Two-Parent	One-Parent	Two-Parent
Interest in national politics				
Interested	32*	20	20	15
Not too interested	68	80	80	85
N	173	173	487	487
Have a partisan preference				
Republicans	9*	5	3	3
Democrats	63	80	74	80
Independents	23	14	20	15
Others	5	1	3	2
N	168	168	488	488
Believe in public control over politicians				
Yes	46	39	37	37
No	54	61	63	63
N	149	149	435	435
Stop government with sit-ins and demonstrations				
Yes	48	40	66	61
No	52	60	34	39
N	149	149	435	435
Stop government by rioting				
Yes	33	27	30	29
No	67	73	70	71
N	156	156	445	445

Source: 1991 Columbus Neighborhood Study Data Set.

*** $p \leq .001$; ** $p \leq .01$; * $p \leq .05$.

influence political communication. The results of the bivariate analyses are listed in Tables 7.7 and 7.8 for whites and blacks. Among poor whites, there were very few substantive or statistically significant differences across family structure in political communication. With the exception of national politics, poor whites overwhelmingly reported that they were involved with people who are interested in local politics and that they discussed politics with family members. Significantly fewer impoverished whites reported discussing politics with church members, co-workers or neighbors, regardless of differences in family structure.

Also contrary to expectations is the finding that the political communication of nonpoor whites was not affected by family structure. A majority of nonpoor whites expressed that the people they know are highly interested in local and national politics. Nonpoor whites in both single-parent and two-parent households were least likely to discuss politics with church members, and most likely to discuss politics with family members. Over 50% of nonpoor whites reported that they discussed politics with co-workers and neighbors.

Consistent with expectations, poor blacks in single-parent and two-parent households reported differences in political communication. Compared with 70% of poor blacks in single-parent households, 86% of poor blacks in two-parent households discussed politics with a family member. Also, while only 44% of poor blacks in single-parent households reported that they discussed politics with a fellow religious worshipper, 62% of poor blacks in two-parent households reported the same. However, poor blacks, regardless of family structure, reported that people they know were interested in local and national politics. Also, less than 30% of poor blacks reported that they discussed politics with coworkers, which may also be related to high levels of unemployment and underemployment. Approximately 50% reported that they discussed politics with neighbors.

Political communication among nonpoor blacks was not substantially impacted by family structure. Over 80% of nonpoor Blacks revealed that their friends are interested in local and national politics. Additionally, despite differences in family structure, a majority of nonpoor blacks report that they discuss politics with family members, co-workers, church members and neighbors.

Table 7.7: Family Structure and Political Communication among Poor and Nonpoor Whites

Responses	Poor Whites		Nonpoor Whites	
	One-Parent	Two-Parent	One-Parent	Two-Parent
People you know interested in local politics				
Interested	75	64	71	68
Not interested	25	36	29	32
N	108	108	444	444
People you know interested in national politics				
Interested	89*	77	87	83
Not interested	21	23	13	17
N	109	109	447	447
Discuss politics with family members				
Yes	81	71	82	82
No	19	29	18	18
N	104	104	423	423
Discuss politics with someone at church				
Yes	20	26	24	30
No	80	74	76	70
N	104	104	422	422
Discuss politics with someone at work				
Yes	23	30	52	60
No	77	70	48	40
N	104	104	420	420
Discuss politics with someone in neighborhood				
Yes	54	53	55	53
No	46	47	45	47
N	104	104	422	422

Source: 1991 Columbus Neighborhood Study Data Set.
*** $p \leq .001$; ** $p \leq .01$; * $p \leq .05$.

Table 7.8: Family Structure and Political Communication among Poor and Nonpoor Blacks

Responses	Poor Whites		Nonpoor Whites	
	One-Parent	Two-Parent	One-Parent	Two-Parent
People you know interested in local politics				
Interested	78	79	84	85
Not interested	22	21	16	15
N	156	156	462	462
People you know interested in national politics				
Interested	80	73	85	84
Not interested	20	27	15	16
N	153	153	459	459
Discuss politics with family members				
Yes	70**	86	80	89
No	30	14	20	11
N	154	154	453	453
Discuss politics with someone at church				
Yes	44**	62	54	61
No	56	38	46	39
N	154	154	451	451
Discuss politics with someone at work				
Yes	28	24	65	57
No	72	76	35	43
N	153	153	446	446
Discuss politics with someone in neighborhood				
Yes	53	54	54	60
No	47	46	46	40
N	155	155	453	453

Source: 1991 Columbus Neighborhood Study Data Set.

***$p \le .001$; **$p \le .01$; *$p \le .05$.

SUMMARY AND DISCUSSION

The foregoing analysis substantiates some aspects of the chapter's hypotheses and disproves others. The first hypothesis, which specified that single-parent households facilitated economic marginalization, is largely borne out by the data. Across racial and income levels, individuals in single-parent households are more likely to receive means-tested government assistance benefits like AFDC and food stamps than individuals in two-parent households. Additionally, they are more likely to rent and less likely to have jobs and automobiles.

The second hypothesis posited that individuals in single-parent households would participate less than individuals in two-parent households. In some instances, family structure influenced participation, especially electoral activities. For example, individuals in single-parent households were less likely to vote than individuals in two-parent households. This finding is extremely important since voting is the primary means of relaying policy preferences to politicians. Earlier analysis in Chapter Seven demonstrated that the economic needs of single-parent households are different from two-parent households. Consequently, the policy preferences of single-parent households are probably not vicariously expressed through the voting of individuals in two-parent households. This means that policy interests of single-parent households, which are in dire need of attention, are probably the least likely to be addressed by policymakers. The findings also revealed that family structure had a more limited influence on non-electoral activities, and unlike electoral participation there were fewer discernable patterns of influences.

Hypothesis two posited that individuals in single-parent households are more likely to harbor negative orientations about the political system than individuals in two-parent households. Overall, there was not a consistent pattern of influences on political orientations. However, individuals in single-parent households were more likely to approve of civil disobedience tactics and identify as independents than their counterparts in two-parent households. These factors suggest that single-parent households are isolated from mainstream political participation and partisan politics and endeavor to use less formal means to effect political change.

Hypothesis three posited that the political communication of single-parent households will be limited as compared with that of two-parent households. The merit of hypothesis three was only borne out among poor blacks in single-parent households, who reported more limited types of political communication than their counterparts in two-parent households. Therefore, while family context had the most profound influences on economic well-being and electoral participation, its influences were least important on political communication.

At this juncture, the focus of the study begins to shift from concerns about the separate influences of family context, neighborhood context and social isolation to concerns about the relative as well as the direct and indirect influences of such factors on political behavior. Providing answers to these important questions is the objective of Chapter Eight.

CHAPTER 8

The Impact of Neighborhoods, Families, and Social Isolation on Political Behavior

... meaningful democratic participation requires that the voices of citizens in politics be clear, loud and equal: clear so that public officials know what citizens want and need, loud so that officials have an incentive to pay attention to what they hear, and equal so that the democratic ideal of equal responsiveness to the preferences and interests of all is not violated. (Verba, Schlozman and Brady, 1995, *Voice and Equality: Civic Volunteerism in American Politics*)

The context of inner-city communities poses many challenges to individuals who desire to participate in electoral and non-electoral activities. These are the individuals whose voices need to be heard by officialdom as loudly as possible. The neighborhood and family structures in which individuals live can either facilitate or hinder access to important social, economic and political resources, which enhance participation in both electoral and non-electoral activities. As Chapters Five, Six, and Seven, respectively, detailed, blacks, whites, poor and nonpoor individuals, who lived in either single-parent or concentrated poverty neighborhoods, were more likely to report dependence on means-tested government assistance, joblessness, and a lack of such basic resources as an automobile and home ownership. In addition to limiting access to social-cum-economic resources, evidence from previous chapters demonstrated that residence in a concentrated poverty neighborhood also facilitates social isolation. Compared with residents in low poverty neighborhoods, black and white residents of concentrated poverty neighborhoods reported lower levels of interaction with upwardly mobile individuals as well as religious and social organizations.

The negative consequences of concentrated poverty neighborhoods also extend to socio-political resources, including interest in political affairs, organizational membership and political communication. For example, residents of concentrated poverty neighborhoods—across race and income categories—were less likely to report interest in political affairs and organizational membership. In a more limited sense, such residents were also less likely to engage in political discussions with neighbors, church members, family members or co-workers. Among poor blacks, residence in single-parent households also stymied political communication. The relevance of these findings for political participation is profound in a variety of ways, especially since all of the foregoing factors—interest in political affairs, institutional involvement, and political communication—are known facilitators of political participation. Lack of access to these important social, economic and political resources causes disadvantages to residents of concentrated poverty neighborhoods and individuals in single-parent households when it comes to political activity.

Since socio-economic and political resources play such a crucial role in mobilizing electoral activities, it is understandable that residence in concentrated poverty neighborhoods as well as single-parent households depressed their involvement in local as well as presidential elections. However, the effects of concentrated poverty neighborhoods were not always negative. In terms of non-electoral activity, residence in impoverished neighborhoods enhanced participation. For example, blacks who lived in concentrated poverty neighborhoods were more likely to attend community meetings than their counterparts who lived in low poverty neighborhoods, while whites who lived in concentrated poverty neighborhoods were more likely to contact political officials. These racial differences in the type of activity that is utilized to affect the policy process speak volumes about differences between whites and blacks in their ability to effect change within the formal structures of power. Very often, blacks utilize external means of rectifying political issues, while whites—of similar socio-economic status—have direct access to the halls of power.

In many respects, the study's findings have gone a long way to highlight the effects of singular contextual forces on a variety of socio-economic and political behaviors. However, inner-city residents do not live in one-dimensional environments; rather their worlds include the simultaneous influences of family and neighborhood contexts as well as a host of other influences. Building on the findings of the previous chapters, the purpose of this chapter is, specifically, to ferret out the relative influences of urban social contexts on the political behavior of white and black inner-city residents. Toward that end, this chapter will review the model presented in Chapter Two and use it to assess the direct and indirect influences of family context, neighborhood context and social isolation on the political behavior of white and black inner-city residents.

As demonstrated in Chapter Two, the model (Figure 8.1) is comprised of eight conceptual factors which can be categorized as either exogenous factors (neighborhood context, family context, income, education and gender) or endogenous (social isolation, socio-political resources and political participation).

MEASURING THE SOCIAL CONTEXT

Neighborhood context, the first exogenous variable, measures the influence of living in poor versus concentrated poverty neighborhoods, while family context measures whether or not individuals live in places that are single-parent versus two-parent households. In addition to the neighborhood- and family-context variables are income, education and gender variables, which researchers have consistently noted for their respective influences on electoral activity.

To the right of the aforementioned variables are the model's endogenous variables. Social isolation measures the extent to which individuals have contact with upwardly mobile individuals who are regularly employed and associated with social and political institutions. The acquisition and mobilization of resources is an important aspect of political participation. For that reason, the model includes four indicators of socio-political resources, including organizational membership, interest in political affairs, church involvement and recruitment.

Through organizational membership, individuals become embedded in social networks that provide politically relevant information as well as the development of political skills. Combined, these benefits of organizational membership diminish the high "costs" of participation in political activities. Moreover, organizational membership places individuals in social networks which reward collective action that furthers group interests. Consequently, individuals who belong to organizations are expected to participate more frequently in political activities than those who report lower levels of organizational involvement (Almond and Verba 1965; Erickson and Nosanchuk 1990; Huckfeldt and Sprague 1987; Obershall 1973; Olson 1965). Additionally, people differ in the psychological resources they bring to politics, but the political participation literature has shown that interest in political affairs consistently fosters electoral participation (Verba and Nie 1972; Tate 1993). Consequently, its role is assessed in the study.

Church activity, which measures the frequency of church attendance, also serves as an important resource for participation in political activities. Political stimuli, within the boundaries of the church, provide a social network which allows individuals to communicate about politically salient issues that, in turn, facilitate action. The black church has historically served as a political entity for the anti-slavery movement, the modern civil rights movement, as well as the current stage of electoral mobilization (Morris 1984). Moreover, the religious right movement, with its promulgation of morality politics in the churches has waged effective battles in local, state and national halls of power (Martin 1996).

Recruitment, which is measured by the number of requests for participation, also plays an important role in stimulating political participation but especially non-electoral activities. Individuals—who are encouraged to participate by either a family member or someone at work, church or in the neighborhood—often report higher levels of political involvement than individuals who are not recruited.

Participation is the ultimate dependent variable, and it is operationalized as electoral activity as well as non-electoral activity.

SOCIAL CONTEXT AND INNER-CITY POLITICAL BEHAVIOR

Contextual theories of political participation, urban poverty research and findings from the previous chapters document the importance of neighborhood and family contextual influences in circumscribing access to social and economic resources. Subsequently, this study posits that these contexts are equally as important in diminishing such politically relevant resources as psychological engagement in politics

Figure 8.1
Theoretical Model

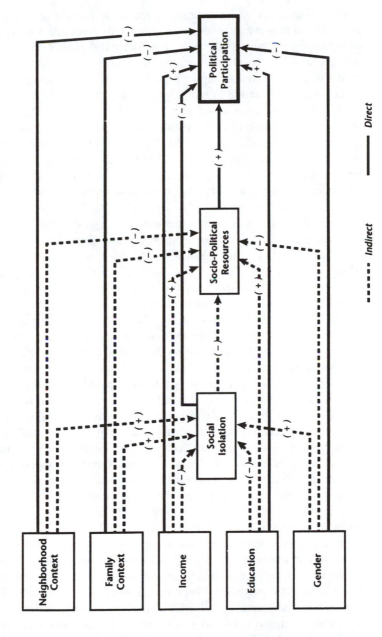

Direct ——— Indirect - - - - -

Neighborhood Context

Family Context

Income

Education

Gender

Social Isolation

Socio-Political Resources

Political Participation

and blocking access to institutions, which are important in facilitating electoral and non-electoral behavior. In spatially isolated, concentrated poverty neighborhoods, where criminal activity, poor neighborhood services and low levels of institutional associations are the norm, residents are expected to report high levels of social isolation. This expectation is denoted in Figure 8.1 by the path arrow which connects neighborhood context with social isolation. The expected consequence of this social isolation is a decrease in socio-political resources. The arrows emanating from the social isolation variable to socio-political resources depict the expected, respective negative relationships. As the arrow which connects socio-political resources to political participation illustrates, the latter are very important facilitators of participation in political activities.

In addition to the indirect influences of neighborhood context on electoral and non-electoral participation, via social isolation and socio-political resources are direct influences. As demonstrated by the arrows which connect neighborhood context to political participation, residence in concentrated poverty neighborhoods is expected to diminish involvement in electoral and non-electoral activities.

As Figure 8.1 also demonstrates, family context is expected to directly and indirectly influence political participation. Previous findings in this study have shown that individuals in single-parent families report higher levels of economic marginalization and social isolation than individuals in two-parent households (Chapter Seven). The arrow connecting family context with social isolation illustrates this expectation. In turn, social isolation is expected to diminish the socio-political resources of individuals in single-parent households. The arrow connecting social isolation with socio-political resources (church involvement, interest in politics, organizational membership and recruitment) illustrates the expected negative relationship. Individuals in single-parent families are faced with a number of challenges— greater psychological stress, frequent changes in employment and residence, greater likelihood of poverty and diminished support systems—which deflect attention away from political interests and decrease opportunities for institutional involvement as well as social networking. In keeping with the political participation literature, lower levels of political interest and institutional involvement are expected to diminish participation in political activities, an expectation that is illustrated by arrows connecting socio-political resources with electoral participation. Additionally, the limited resources of individuals in single-parent households are expected to limit participation in electoral as well as non-electoral activities.

In addition to the contextual factors listed above, income, education and gender are expected to directly and indirectly affect the political participation of inner-city residents. Individuals with higher levels of income and education are expected to report lower levels of social isolation than those who are less affluent and educated, while women are expected to report higher levels of social isolation than men. Additionally, income, education and gender are expected to affect socio-political resources. Individuals with higher levels of income and education, however, are expected to exhibit higher levels of psychological engagement than their counterparts who earn less money and possess fewer educational credentials. The arrows connecting income with socio-political resources (interest in politics, church involvement, organizational membership, and recruitment) depict the foregoing expectations. In keeping with gender literature on institutional involvement, religious involvement and interest in political affairs, gender is expected to have a mixed influence on socio-political resources. For example, women are expected to be more involved in religious and social organizations than their male counterparts but less psychologically engaged in political issues than men (Verba, Schlozman and Brady 1995).

The results of Chapter Six have demonstrated the differentiating influences of neighborhood context on political behavior. Concentrated poverty neighborhoods catalyze involvement in non-electoral activities, while they depress involvement in electoral activities. Therefore, it is necessary to separately compute and analyze models for electoral and non-electoral activity. In a large measure, however, the components of both models are the same, with one important distinction: Recruitment, which is defined as encouragement to participate in political activities—is included as a component of socio-political resources for the non-electoral model, but it is not included as an indicator of socio-political resources for the electoral model. The reason for this distinction lies in the fact that non-electoral activities, in contrast to electoral activities, are frequently communal and socially based, and, therefore, the latter are more subject to recruitment than the former. As a result, non-electoral activity is often prompted by requests from political elites, family members or individuals at work, in the neighborhood or at church. In keeping with the findings from previous chapters, individuals in single-parent households and concentrated poverty neighborhoods are expected to receive fewer recruitment appeals than their counterparts in more mainstream neighborhood and family environments.

Race is also an important component of the model and, as the study's findings have demonstrated, it is inextricably tied to the cauldron of inner-city contexts. To a large extent, therefore, the influences of inner-city neighborhoods, families and social isolation are expected to depress the electoral activities of blacks and whites alike. However, the influences are expected to be more profound for blacks, since structural changes in the economy, transformation in neighborhood contexts and racial-cum-class segregation have disproportionately affected African American communities. Toward that end, separate models will be computed for whites and blacks, respectively, with tests for racial differences.

Consistent with the theoretical thrust of the study are five hypotheses which are delineated below:

1. Concentrated poverty neighborhoods and single-parent households facilitate social isolation.

2. Social isolation diminishes socio-political resources that facilitate political participation. The higher the level of social isolation, the lower the levels of religious involvement, interest in politics, organizational membership and, in the case of non-electoral activities, recruitment.

3. Concentrated poverty neighborhoods and single-parent households decrease socio-political resources. Individuals who reside in concentrated poverty neighborhoods and single-parent households are expected to attend church less frequently, report lower levels of interest in political affairs, lower levels of involvement in organizations and fewer recruitment opportunities to become involved in non-electoral activities.

4. Concentrated poverty neighborhoods, single-parent households and social isolation diminish participation in electoral and non-electoral activities.

5. The effects of concentrated poverty neighborhoods, single-parent households and social isolation are expected to be more acute among inner-city blacks than whites because of the enduring legacy of racial discrimination and segregation that African Americans have faced.

A series of ordinary least-square regression equations and a logistic regression equation are utilized to test the foregoing hypotheses. A more detailed explanation of the methodology is presented in Appendix B, while a detailed explanation of the concepts is presented in Appendix A.

POLITICAL BEHAVIOR IN INNER-CITY COMMUNITIES

Hypothesis One: Concentrated Poverty Neighborhoods and Single-Parent Households Facilitate Social Isolation Among Black and White Inner-City Residents

In a large measure, the expectations of hypothesis one are borne out by the results in Table 8.1. Whites in single-parent households and concentrated poverty neighborhoods are much more likely to report social isolation than their counterparts in two-parent households. Among blacks, the effects of living in single-parent households have a negligible impact on social isolation. This is probably due to the complex coping mechanisms that black women have constructed to deal with the high levels of female-headed households in the black community (Stack 1974). However, residence in concentrated poverty neighborhoods is statistically associated with higher levels of social isolation, which illuminates the lack of access to individuals with connections to mainstream institutions. Not only are such upwardly mobile individuals important in job searches, but they also serve as excellent role models for political participation.

Hypothesis Two: Social Isolation Diminishes Socio-Political Resources

Contrary to expectations, social isolation has a limited effect on the socio-political resources of inner-city residents (Table 8.2). Among whites, the effects of social isolation on socio-political resources are small and statistically insignificant. Among blacks, the effects of social isolation are limited to organizational membership and interest in political affairs. As shown in Table 8.2, blacks who report limited contact with upwardly mobile individuals underscore lower levels of interest in political affairs as well as lower levels of organizational

Table 8.1

Social Isolation among Whites and Blacks with Statistical Tests for
Racial Differences

	Social Isolation		
	Whites	Blacks	Diff.
Neighborhood Context	.588***	.353*	−.235
Family Context	.660**	.197	−.464
Income	.224**	−.002	−.225*
Education	−.101	.095	.196
Gender	.175	.329*	.154
Constant	258	−.003	
Adjusted R^2	−250.2	290.3	
N	414	421	

***$p \leq .01$; **$p \leq .05$; *$p \leq .10$

membership. However, social isolation does not influence religious
involvement or recruitment activities of blacks.

**Hypothesis Three: Concentrated Poverty Neighborhoods and
Single-Parent Households Erode Socio-Political Resources**

The results in Table 8.2 provide mixed assessment of the validity of
hypothesis three. Among blacks, the effects of neighborhood context on
socio-political resources are small and statistically insignificant.
However, the influence of family context proves to be important in
terms of religious involvement and interest in political affairs—two
socio-political resources which are important facilitators of both
electoral and non-electoral activities. Among blacks, residence in
single-parent households leads to a .238 standard deviation decrease in
church attendance.

Residence in single-parent families not only impacts involvement
in religious institutions, but it also has a debilitating effect on interest in
political affairs (Table 8.2). Residence in single-parent households
decreases interest in political affairs among blacks by .128 standard
deviations. This is particularly unfortunate since the political
participation literature is replete with studies which have demonstrated
how individuals who are interested in political affairs are more likely to
participate in both electoral and non-electoral activities than those who
report less interest.

Table 8.2: Socio-Political Resources among Whites and Blacks with Statistical Tests for Racial Differences

	Religious Involvement			Political Interest			Organizational Membership			Recruitment		
	Whites	Blacks	Diff.	Whites	Blacks	Diff.	Whites	Blacks	Diff.	Whites	Blacks	Diff.
Neighborhood Context	-.244**	.024	.268	.006	-.060	-.054	-.074	.114	.188	.232**	.029	-.204
Family Context	-.183*	.238***	-.054	.031	-.128*	-.159	.113	.125	.012	.086	-.006	-.092
Income	-.114*	-.042	.072	.120**	.123***	.069	.065	.245***	.180***	.152***	.061	-.091
Education	.181***	-.020	-.201***	.153***	.223***	.069	-.012	.262***	.235*	.060	.056	-.004
Gender	.376***	.443***	.067	.060	.050	-.111	.008			-.101	.084	.186
Social Isolation	-.114	.102	.215*	.070	-.210***	-.280**	-.132	-.204**	-.072	.029	.163***	-.132**
Religious Involvement				.084**	-.039	-.123**	.221***	.365***	.144**	.211***	.193***	-.019
Political Interest							.084*	.225***	.141**	.054	.064*	.011
Organizational Membership												
Recruitment												
Constant	-.341	-.029		-.036	.474		.017	.003		-.108	-.074	
Adjusted R²	.064	.076		.073	.093		.144	.127		.092	.047	
N	359	421		359	419		359	419		359	419	

*** $p \leq .001$; ** $p \leq .01$; * $p \leq .05$.

Among whites, the effects of neighborhood context and family context in eroding socio-political resources are most evident with religious involvement. One standard deviation increase in poverty decreases religious involvement among whites by .244 standard deviations. Additionally, residence in a single-parent family context results in a .183 standard deviation decrease in religious involvement. Limited involvement in church activities is politically disadvantageous as morality politics as well as the political maturation of the religious right demonstrate the importance of white Protestant churches as sites for the transmission of political mobilization and civic skills.

In addition to the influence of neighborhood context on religious involvement is the statistically significant relationship between neighborhood context and recruitment (Table 8.2). Among whites, residence in concentrated poverty neighborhoods increases recruitment. One standard deviation increase in poverty is associated with a .232 increase in recruitment or encouragement to participate in political activities. While inconsistent with expectations, the finding is neither implausible nor inexplicable. In fact, its relevance is linked to the strong neighborhood associations which are an integral part of the Columbus, Ohio, city government. As detailed in Chapter Three, citizens utilize these associations to engage in face-to-face democracy. They contact political officials, attend community meetings, and actually participate in zoning and other development issues. As a result, it is not surprising that the analysis implicitly demonstrates the efficacy of these associations in stimulating participation even in the concentrated poverty neighborhoods. It is also not surprising that concentrated poverty neighborhoods facilitated recruitment among whites but not blacks. This is especially so since earlier analyses showed that whites were more likely to report that they contacted political officials, who are known to recruit citizens for political involvement. Additionally, studies have demonstrated that blacks in concentrated poverty neighborhoods are subject to much higher levels of discrimination than their white counterparts. The harsher form of segregation and social isolation among blacks impedes the formation of social networks which are necessary for recruitment.

Furthermore, the finding of higher levels of recruitment among whites in concentrated poverty neighborhoods is consistent with some previous research on neighborhood politics. Other studies have demonstrated that in neighborhoods which are beleaguered by social and economic problems, there is often a higher level of recruitment or encouragement to participate in non-electoral activities which are aimed at catalyzing change from outside the formal political process (Berry, Portney and Thomson 1991; Crenson 1983).

Contrary to expectations, however, the influences of neighborhood context and family context, respectively, on other forms of socio-political resources—including interest in political affairs and organizational membership—are minimal and statistically insignificant.

Hypothesis Four: Concentrated Poverty Neighborhoods and Single-Parent Households Undermine Participation in Electoral and Non-Electoral Activities

The three previous hypotheses have largely assessed the indirect influences of concentrated poverty neighborhoods and single-parent households on political participation via social isolation and socio-political resources. Hypothesis Four attempts to assess the direct impacts of concentrated poverty neighborhoods and single-parent households on the electoral and non-electoral participation of inner-city whites and blacks. The results are delineated in Table 8.3.

As expected, residence in concentrated poverty neighborhoods and single-parent households decreases the electoral activities of whites above and beyond the influences of income and education. One standard deviation increase in concentrated poverty decreases electoral participation among whites by .162 standard deviations, while living in single-parent households decreases electoral participation by .167 standard deviations.

Table 8.1 demonstrated strong relationships between social isolation and neighborhood and family contexts, respectively. The expectation was that social isolation would limit access to socio-political resources and depress participation in both electoral and non-electoral activities. However, the findings in Table 8.3 havedemonstrated that social isolation has very little predictive capability vis-à-vis the electoral activities of whites. Instead, the beta weight is small, indicating that the influence of social isolation on electoral activities among whites is insignificant.

Human capital characteristics exert important influences on the electoral activities of whites. One standard deviation increase in education elevates electoral activity by .100 standard deviations. Moreover, the findings buttress recent gender literature which shows that the gender gap in political participation has significantly closed. In

Table 8.3: Electoral and Nonelectoral Activities among Whites and Blacks with Statistical Tests for Racial Differences

	Electoral Activity			Non-Electoral Activity		
	Whites	Blacks	Diff.	Whites	Blacks	Diff.
Neighborhood Context	-.162**	-.102	.059	.030	.013	-.017
Family Context	-.167*	-.046	.122	.153*	.084	-.069
Income	-.074*	.013	.086	.055	.041	-.013
Education	.100**	-.063	-.163***	.069**	.115**	.046
Gender	.138*	.067	-.071	.006	-.029	-.035
Social Isolation	-.023	-.145**	-.118	.023	-.074	-.098
Religious Involvement	.108***	.124***	.016	-.071**	.079*	.151***
Political Interest	.366***	.315***	-.051	.248***	.271***	.024
Organizational Membership	.195***	.052*	-.142**	.265***	.138***	-.117**
Recruitment				.552***	.434***	-.118**
Constant	-.110	.287		-.014	-.008	
Adjusted R²	.190	.159		.450	.419	
N	359	418		359	419	

*** $p \le .001$; ** $p \le .01$; * $p \le .05$.

fact, white women are more likely than their male counterparts to report participation in electoral activities. The negative relationship between income and electoral activity among whites is odd but not inexplicable. Traditionally, income has exerted a positive influence on electoral activity, whereby higher levels of income are associated with higher levels of electoral participation. However, research has also demonstrated that higher-status individuals who reside in a low-status context are sometimes less likely to participate because of the incongruence between individual status and social context (Huckfeldt 1986).

Among blacks, the effects of neighborhood context and family context on electoral activity are substantively small and statistically insignificant. In contrast, social isolation exerts a strong influence on the electoral activities. Among blacks who report limited interaction with upwardly mobile individuals, electoral activity is diminished by .145 standard deviations. The effect of social isolation on electoral activity is, in fact, the second strongest influence on the electoral activities among blacks. The finding suggests that while scholars have extolled the deleterious effects of neighborhood context on political participation, they have missed a very important but rarely assessed aspect of the current urban social milieu—the lack of contact between impoverished inner-city residents and upwardly mobile individuals. As a result of failing to control for the impact of social isolation, previous studies may have overestimated the influence of contextual factors on social as well as political behavior of inner-city residents.

At the same time the findings underscore the important role that socio-political resources like religious involvement, political interests and organizational membership play in facilitating electoral activities among whites and blacks. Among whites, religious involvement, organizational membership and interest in political affairs catalyze electoral participation. One standard deviation increase in religious involvement leads to a .108 increase in electoral participation; one standard deviation increase in interest in political affairs is associated with a .366 increase in electoral participation, and one standard deviation increase in organizational membership is related to a .195 increase in electoral participation.

With the exception of religious involvement, which decreases non-electoral participation among whites by .071 standard deviations, the salutary effects of socio-political resources are also evident on non-electoral participation. For example, one standard deviation increase in political interest leads to a .248 increase in non-electoral participation; one standard deviation increase in organizational membership elevates non-electoral participation by .256 standard deviations and one standard deviation increase in recruitment increases non-electoral participation by .552 standard deviations.

Similar patterns of relationships are evident among blacks with respect to electoral activity. One-standard deviation increase in religious involvement corresponds to a .124 increase in electoral participation, while one standard deviation increase in political interests elevates electoral participation among blacks by .315 standard deviations. Organizational membership also facilitates black electoral activity as one standard deviation increase in organizational involvement leads to a .052 increase in electoral participation.

Among whites, the relationship between contextual factors and non-electoral activities contrasts significantly with the findings for electoral activities. The coefficient for neighborhood context is small and statistically insignificant. Contrary to expectations, therefore, there is no relationship between neighborhood context and participation in non-electoral activities.

The relationship between family context and non-electoral participation is statistically significant, and the findings suggest that residence in single-parent households increases participation in non-electoral activities. This finding contravenes expectations and suggests that relative deprivation might propel individuals in such single-parent contexts to participate at higher levels than are expected as a way of compensating for and possibly ameliorating the difficulties of single-parent households.

Human capital characteristics play a limited role in facilitating non-electoral activities among whites. The effects of income and gender are small and statistically insignificant, while the effects of education are small but statistically significant. One standard deviation increase in education elevates non-electoral participation among whites by .069 standard deviations.

Among blacks, the coefficients for neighborhood context and family context, respectively, are small and statistically insignificant, which suggests that blacks' participation in non-electoral activities is unaffected by family structure or the level of neighborhood poverty. The findings also demonstrated that social isolation has little impact on the non-electoral activities of blacks. Instead, the most important influences include socio-political resources. The higher the levels of religious involvement, interest in political affairs, organizational membership and recruitment, the higher the level of participation in non-electoral activities. Similar to the findings among whites, recruitment exerts the strongest influence among socio-political resources on the non-electoral activities of blacks. One standard deviation increase in recruitment leads to .434 standard deviation increases in the non-electoral participation of blacks. This finding unequivocally demonstrates the importance of social networks as crucial not only to socio-economic mobility but to political involvement as well.

The results in Table 8.3 also demonstrate the cumulative effects of socio-political resources on the electoral and non-electoral activities of whites and blacks. Unfettered access to one socio-political resource facilitates access to others. For example, among whites and blacks, one standard deviation increase in religious involvement is associated with .221 and .365 increases, respectively, in organizational membership. Whites and blacks who attend church are more likely to belong to other organizations, than their counterparts who attend church less frequently. Additionally, whites and blacks who report membership in organizations are more likely to report recruitment activities than their counterparts who are less involved in social institutions.

While these findings are interesting and somewhat crucial in their own right, it is important to emphasize their connection with the broader goals of the study. Indeed, the implications of the findings suggest that debilitating effects of neighborhood context and family context not only impede access to a specific socio-political resource like religious involvement, but that they also hinder inner-city residents from acquiring other socio-political resources which play an important role in facilitating participation in electoral and non-electoral activities.

Hypothesis Five: The Effects of Neighborhood Context, Family Context and Social Isolation Are More Debilitating for Blacks Than Whites

As the coefficients delineated in Table 8.3 and Figures 8.2, 8.3, 8.4 and 8.5 illustrate, the effects of neighborhood context and family context were more important in depressing the electoral and non-electoral activities of whites (Figures 8.2 and 8.3) than blacks (Figures 8.4 and 8.5), while the effect of social isolation was more detrimental to the electoral activity of blacks than whites. These findings are particularly interesting, because heretofore, the impact of concentrated poverty neighborhoods and single-parent households had not been analyzed in a comparative fashion. Instead, researchers always assumed that the aforementioned factors were only important for blacks who were concentrated in inner-city communities.

In addition to omitting whites from most analyses of inner-city political participation, researchers also rarely examined the consequences of social isolation as a separate phenomenon from neighborhood context. Instead, researchers always assumed that residents were socially isolated by virtue of their residence in concentrated poverty neighborhoods. However, this study has demonstrated that the spatial or geographic isolation of concentrated poverty neighborhoods is different from the social isolation that residents face and that it is important to independently examine the role of social isolation as a viable and separate phenomenon. Indeed, the analysis suggests that while context is important in undermining the political participation of whites, social isolation is most important in undermining the political participation of blacks (Figures 8.4 and 8.5).

At the same time, it is important to underscore that the noted racial differences in the effects of neighborhood context, family context or social isolation variables on political participation are not statistically significant. Instead, the findings have demonstrated that the most important racial differences are evident with respect to socio-political resources. Without exception, the electoral and non-electoral activity of whites (Figures 8.2 and 8.3; Table 8.3) receives a greater boost from socio-political resources than blacks (Figures 8.4 and 8.5; Table 8.3). The effects are especially significant with non-electoral activity whereby the differences are large enough to reach statistical significance (Figures 8.3 and 8.5). With the exception of religious activity, the non-electoral activity of whites is catalyzed to a greater extent by political interest, organizational membership and recruitment than blacks. These findings are especially significant since concentrated poverty neighborhoods, family context and social isolation depress socio-political resources of whites and blacks and thus, indirectly, affect both electoral and non-electoral participation.

DISCUSSION AND CONCLUSION

Most discussions of political participation in America are based on national samples, with only scant attention devoted to issues of context,

Electoral Activity
Figures 8.2–8.5

Figure 8.2
White Electoral Activity

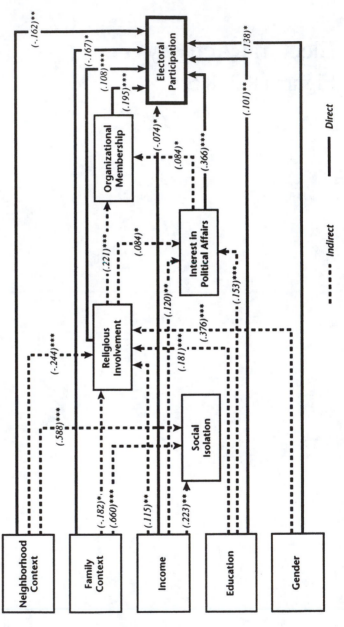

***p ≤ .01; **p ≤.05; *p ≤.10

Figure 8.3
Non-electoral Participation Among Whites

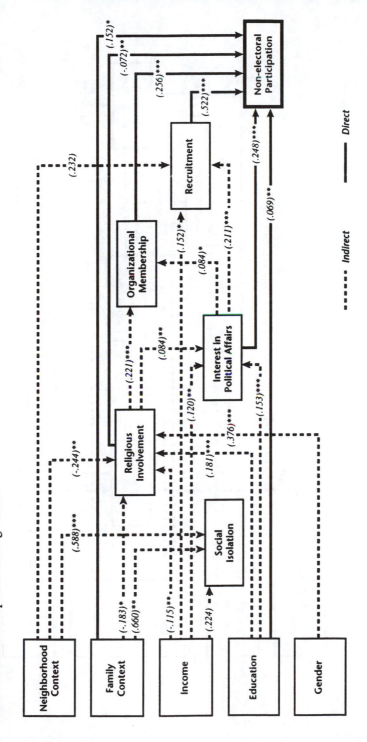

***p ≤ .01; **p ≤ .05; *p ≤ .10

Figure 8.4
Black Electoral Activity

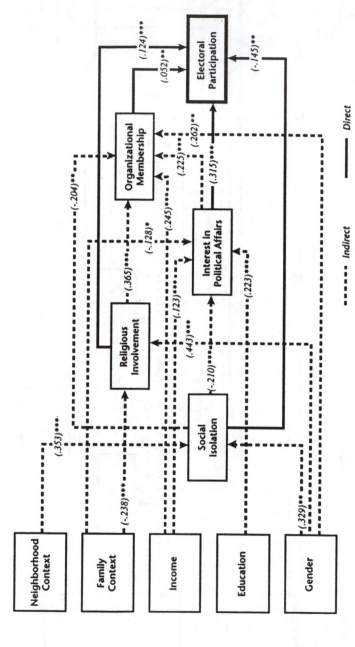

***$p \le .01$; **$p \le .05$; *$p \le .10$

Figure 8.5
Non-electoral Participation Among Blacks

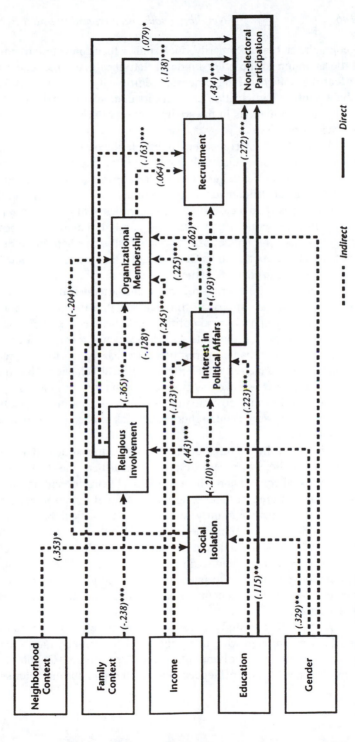

***p ≤ .01; **p ≤ .05; *p ≤ .10

geography and race. Primarily, such studies focus on voting trends with little attention to the other kinds of activities that Americans use to affect the policy-making process. Additionally, very little is known about political participation in inner-city communities and the extent to which transformations in the social context of urban America impede participatory efforts.

In an effort to offer answers to this glaring omission in the political behavior literature, this study articulated and tested a multivariate causal model of electoral and non-electoral participation with statistical tests for racial differences among whites and blacks. Although the analysis is based on a case study of Columbus, Ohio, the single-parent households, economic indicators and concentrated poverty neighborhoods are typical of the trends that are present in other mid-western and east coast cities. Consequently, the results are applicable to many other urban contexts in the United States.

As a result of exploring primarily uncharted terrain, the study has unearthed several empirical findings which have implications for theories of urban poverty and political participation. The study has been helpful in advancing the state of urban poverty theory and research. Heretofore, the urban poverty literature has primarily ignored the implications of inner-city contexts for political behavior. The findings for this study have shown that political behavior is definitely impacted by the debilitating circumstances of single-parent households, concentrated poverty neighborhoods, the lack of adequate resources and social isolation.

Certainly, the findings unequivocally demonstrated that context matters. While prior research has unearthed the link between neighborhood context and a host of political behavior and orientations, this study ventured further along the contextual terrain to explore the relationship between family structure and political behavior. The findings demonstrated that the impact of family context varies across modes of political participation and that single-parent households lacked access to important socio-political resources. These findings are extremely relevant as the phenomenon of single-parent households moves from a rarity to a common structural arrangement in the twenty-first century.

Above all, the study is important in its efforts to explain the mechanisms through which neighborhood context and family context depress political involvement. As the results of Chapter Eight demonstrated, these influences operate through the mechanisms of social isolation and by limiting access to socio-political resources, which facilitate involvement in both electoral and non-electoral activities.

In fact, the importance of resources as facilitators of political participation has received a great deal of attention in the recent political behavior literature. A majority of the work has focused on how deficits in human capital characteristics diminish the availability of socio-political or civic resources. However, this study demonstrated that social isolation, neighborhood context and family context exerted primarily negative influences on socio-political resources, above and beyond the influences of such human capital characteristics as income and education. Relatedly, political participation research has traditionally shown that the poor participate less because of lower levels of socio-economic status characteristics. This study shed light on the fact that the poor are not only disadvantaged by limited income and educational factors but also by deleterious contextual environments as well.

The study also reaffirmed the importance of differentiating between electoral and non-electoral participation as well as the importance of strong neighborhood associations in facilitating face-to-face democracy. Among whites, concentrated poverty neighborhoods diminished involvement in electoral activities. On the other hand, single-parent households enhanced non-electoral participation and concentrated poverty neighborhoods enhanced recruitment, whereby whites in concentrated poverty neighborhoods were more likely to be encouraged to participate than individuals in low poverty neighborhoods. The relationship between neighborhood context and recruitment is important because, as the findings show, recruitment had the most potent influence on non-electoral activities. These findings lend support to recent studies which have shown that political structures—especially strong neighborhood associations with connections to municipal government—can provide citizens with the motivations and stimuli to participate in the political process, even in the midst of stifling poverty.

Among blacks, contextual factors have no direct influences on either electoral or non-electoral participation. This finding contradicts an earlier study which characterized the deleterious consequences of concentrated poverty neighborhoods on African American political behavior. The previous study did not assess the role of social isolation, which may have inflated the effects of concentrated poverty neighborhoods on political behavior. After all, the findings in this study clearly demonstrate that social isolation significantly lowers electoral involvement among blacks. Its effect on non-electoral activity, in contrast, is indirect through the mechanism of socio-political resources. Moreover, socio-political resources—with the exception of church involvement—are more beneficial in enhancing the political participation among whites than blacks. The lack of connection with upwardly mobile individuals not only impairs the ability of blacks to find suitable employment, but it also hinders their ability to participate in the political process. Induced by the debilitating circumstances of concentrated poverty neighborhoods and single-parent households, social isolation renders blacks—who desperately need to have their voices heard through the mechanisms of voting—mute and incapable of effecting change in the political process. In this respect, the findings of this study have also contributed to a deeper understanding of how race as well as class factors explain urban poverty.

In discussing the phenomenon of the urban underclass, Wilson and other scholars emphasize the importance of class issues and contextual factors in facilitating the problems of inner-city residents. They have argued that concentration effects or environmental factors and not race lead to the so-called underclass behavior. Since all of the prior studies were based on a uni-racial sample of blacks, there was no definitive, empirical assessment of these claims. The results presented in Chapter Four of this work, however, demonstrated that many of the social and economic behavioral problems that are associated with inner-city blacks are not race specific. In many respects, the findings delineated in Chapter Four challenge researchers to analyze the issue of urban poverty as well as the correlates of single-parent households and concentrated poverty neighborhoods not as a "black" or "minority" problem but as an issue that is problematic for all of American society. In this respect, the study's findings have provided evidence to substantiate Wilson's claims about the importance of class as well as contextual factors in impeding the socio-economic mobility of Americans, regardless of race.

At the same time, the findings—especially those presented in Chapter Eight—challenge the notion that either contemporary or historical racial factors should be de-emphasized as important explanatory variables of urban poverty. The evidence in Chapter Eight demonstrated how the lack of access to resources limited electoral and non-electoral participation among blacks. The findings also demonstrated that politically relevant resources were more efficacious in the political involvement of whites vis-à-vis blacks. Evidence from interviews with neighborhood leaders—as detailed in Chapter Three—also illustrated the importance of race. Neighborhood leaders in the predominantly white working-class and concentrated poverty neighborhoods reported more access to political resources and officials than their counterparts in predominantly black neighborhoods. Moreover, leaders in the predominantly white neighborhoods identified their relationships with political leaders as extremely important in gaining the needed resources for their respective neighborhoods.

These findings indicate that while Wilson's concept of the urban underclass was important in the "re-discovery" of urban poverty, it has not sufficiently captured the complexity and diversity of America's urban population. Above all, the findings illustrate that even when whites and blacks share similar circumstances of individual and contextual impoverishment, the enduring legacy of racial discrimination as well as its contemporary machinations impedes black access to important socio-economic and political resources. Therefore, while whites and blacks may suffer similarly from urban poverty issues, whites seem to be more advantaged because of access to politically relevant resources as well as their position in important social and political networks.

In a large measure, the findings echo the arguments of the Verba, Schlozman and Brady study, which emphasized the existence of participation inequalities, whereby citizens with greater resources participated more than those with fewer resources. However, an important finding of this study is that the lack of resources is not merely the result of inequalities in individual or human capital characteristics but, most importantly, the result of contextual-cum-structural inequities. Chapter Nine will explore the implications of these findings for democracy and political participation among low-income, as well as more affluent citizens.

CHAPTER 9

National Urban Policy and Political Behavior in Inner-City Communities

How in the name of American democracy can we say to Eastern Europe that democratic capitalism will work there if we can't make it work in East L.A. or East Harlem or East Palo Alto, California. . . . Civility cannot return to our country unless every person feels they have an equal shot at the American dream. Jack Kemp, 1996 vice presidential nominee at the vice presidential debate, Mahaffey Theater, Petersburg, Virginia (*The Richmond Times Dispatch*, October 10, 1996)

INTRODUCTION

The preceding eight chapters have assessed the impact of the urban social context on the political behavior of white and black inner-city residents and shown that, with respect to voting, residence in inner-city communities diminishes voting as well as access to politically relevant resources which enhance voting. However, the debilitating context of inner-city communities does not only limit the involvement of individual citizens in local politics, it is also associated with the waning political influence of cities. Compared to the 1940s, when urban residents constituted almost 30% of the electorate in presidential campaigns, they comprised a mere 14% of the national vote in 1992. Steep declines in voter participation among urban residents is also apparent in state-wide elections. In New York, for example, voter participation among city residents witnessed a 20% decline since the 1940s (Judd and Swanstrom, forthcoming).

As this chapter will demonstrate, federal urban legislation has played an important role in either facilitating or obstructing citizen participation in politics. While a comprehensive discussion of national urban policy is beyond the parameters of this book, the final chapter will show how some federal mandates during the 1960s and 1970s encouraged participation. In stark contrast, the 1980s were marked by a vigorous attempt to de-regulate and discourage citizen participation in urban decision-making. About 30 years after the War on Poverty was declared, many of America's urban citizens still languish in the sweltering heat of poverty and oppression, where according to vice presidential nominee Jack Kemp, citizens have not experienced the virtues of democratic capitalism. As a consequence, urban residents in the 1990s have questioned the legitimacy of urban government and engaged in a variety of attempts from urban uprisings to strategies of succession. The chapter concludes with an assessment of these participatory strategies for the practice of democracy in urban America.

WAR ON POVERTY: THE MODERN FOUNDATIONS OF URBAN CITIZEN POLITICAL PARTICIPATION

By all credible estimates, the decade of the 1960s marks the modern foundation of urban citizen participation in politics. Convinced that federal action was necessary to eliminate poverty and other social ills, President Lyndon B. Johnson called for a War on Poverty. An integral aspect of the battle plan called for the empowerment of previously disfranchised members of society, especially inner-city residents, racial minorities and the poor. Under the rubric of the War on Poverty, the federal government worked directly with organizations and leaders to provide resources and encourage participation in and support for Democrats in subsequent elections. Prodded by the growing strength of the Civil Rights movement and a calculation that political parties could benefit from appealing to black voters, the Democrats forged a successful campaign on resolving the issues of urban crises, which included problems of racial segregation and concentrated poverty.

The most visible manifestation of the Johnson administration's efforts to empower the poor occurred in 1964 with the passage of the Economic Opportunity Act, which authorized the creation of

Community Action Programs (CAP) and required the "maximum feasible participation" of the poor in locally developed community action programs. Local community action agencies, which were established as part of CAP were charged with the responsibility of actively involving the poor in the implementation of community programs. With the establishment of these programs and organizations, the federal government provided an opportunity for the poor to be involved in shaping the policies and institutions that affected their lives. Additionally, the riots of the mid-1960s provided a source of circumstantial proof that government officials needed to include the poor in policy-making decisions and engage in efforts to redistribute wealth and power in American society.

Assessments and evaluations of the War on Poverty and Great Society efforts, respectively, varied. Many previously disfranchised individuals saw the Community Action Programs as an effort by the federal government to live up to its promises of democracy by dismantling the impediments that thwarted participation among the poor. In contrast, many bureaucrats and city officials envisioned the Community Action Programs as a necessary evil that had to be tolerated in order to acquire federal funds. Problems also arose because of the lack of experience that many community members had in organizing community programs and the unwillingness of many city officials to assist officials in poor communities in organizing constituents. In spite of the problems that arose as a result of government's efforts to facilitate citizen participation in local policy-making, there is evidence that the War on Poverty witnessed a decrease in the poverty rate among American citizens. In 1960, the poverty rate was 22%, but by the end of the War on Poverty campaign, the national poverty rate had been cut in half to a rate of 11% (Judd and Swanstrom, forthcoming).

Additionally, the Model Cities Programs provided citizens with the opportunity to participate in local governance by mandating that neighborhood organizations were supposed to either provide city governments with either approval or disapproval of proposals that affected geographical areas. To facilitate this process, residents were elected to Model Cities Commissions, which served as liaisons between city government and residents. The 1970s witnessed a continued expansion of federal mandates for citizen participation including involvement in such areas as the environment, education and community development. The federal government also required citizen participation in General Revenue Sharing Programs which required various aspects of local government to include citizens in the decision-making process of allocating monies.

THE BACKLASH AGAINST CITIZEN PARTICIPATION

While the 1960s and 1970s witnessed increased federal efforts to encourage citizen participation in politics and the empowerment of previously disfranchised poor citizens in the policy-making process, the late 1970s and the entire decade of the 1980s were characterized by the institutionalization and outright discouragement of citizen participation in local policy-making. This change in federal efforts to involve citizens was a result of an intersection of forces at the urban and federal levels. At the urban level, many cities including Detroit, Cleveland, and New York were experiencing fiscal crises which were attributed to the over-participation of local citizens in the urban policy-making and the concomitant demand for services. In the wake of fiscal crises, many urban officials de-emphasized citizen participation and focused instead on urban entrepreneurship as a means of attracting capital investments to local communities.

At the national level, the 1980s marked the beginning of the Reagan administration with its priorities of fiscal conservatism. President Reagan deemed federal regulation of citizen participation expensive and unnecessary. Above all, such participatory efforts were perceived as crafty avenues for empowering and mobilizing liberal and community activists who would undermine the authority of duly elected urban officials. Specifically, the programs were thought to create too much access to decision-making for the poor and for racial as well as ethnic minorities at the expense of the white middle class (Berry, Portney and Thomson 1993). As a result, the Reagan administration worked vigorously to de-regulate, modify and, in some instances, eliminate citizen participation requests from federal legislation. During the 1980s, bureaucrats buttressed these efforts in their lax monitoring of local participation requirements.

The Reagan administration's efforts at de-regulation were not limited to citizen participation but also included civil rights legislation (Walton 1988). While the de-regulation of civil rights policies did not begin with Reagan, the process was accelerated under his tenure. Pleased with the de-regulation of civil rights requirements in the Department of Housing and Urban Development, which was responsible for enforcing fair housing laws, the Reagan administration encouraged similar de-regulation in the Department of Education (Walton 1988). Ultimately, the de-regulation meant that the states would be responsible for administering programs and that the federal government would not be responsible for mediating civil rights grievances (Walton 1988). Since rules, regulation and enforcement policies vary across states, the impact of civil rights de-regulation was that the gains made by the 1960s Civil Rights movement for minorities were jeopardized, especially among impoverished urban residents, who are most in need of political-cum-economic justice (Walton 1988).

President Ronald Reagan's attack on citizen participation was an integral part of his administration's emphasis on the trickle-down theory of economics, which posited that cities must create conducive business climates, which will, in turn, attract private investments and lead to business prosperity, jobs and rising land values. According to the trickle-down theory, these factors lead to a healthy tax base which will allow citizens to obtain necessary municipal services. An important aspect of the trickle-down theory was its vigorous efforts at de-regulation and the concomitant absence of citizen participation in urban policy-making decisions.

LIMITED CITIZEN INVOLVEMENT AND URBAN POLICY-MAKING IN THE 1980S

Based on this logic, the Reagan administration encouraged mayors and other city officials to cut municipal taxes and offer tax abatements and other incentives to spur growth. In the absence of organized citizen efforts, many urban areas created enterprise zones as a solution for urban blight. In line with the emphasis on creating a conducive climate for economic activity, businesses in these "enterprise" zones would have 75% or more of their corporate income tax forgiven, no capital gains tax, no tariffs or duties in areas also designated by the federal government as free trade zones; employers would be given tax credits—an attempt at promoting economic growth in the inner cities. However, in many instances, the economic benefits and profits reaped in inner-city enterprise zones bypassed inner-city residents, who were often ill equipped to take advantage of highly skilled employment opportunities. Instead, the profits lined the pockets of suburban residents who trekked in to urban areas to take advantage of employment opportunities and trekked out with the earned salaries, without contributing much to the city tax base. In the end, cities lost more in terms of increased expenditures for city services (sanitation, police, infrastructure) than they gained in terms of employment benefits and improved standard of living for urban residents.

With limited involvement of citizens in the policy-making decisions of mayors, the priorities of trickle-down economics went a long way to accelerate urban inequalities as well as the patterns of unequal development within cities. In fact, it is important to underscore that social scientists pinpoint the initial increase in concentrated poverty neighborhoods during the late 1970s, with continued proliferation during the 1980s—time periods that coincide with a reduction and subsequent elimination of federal efforts to encourage citizen participation in urban decision-making. The effects of limited citizen involvement and increased dependence on the business sector are documented in the statement below:

> Among the more intangible yet clearly most consequential costs have been a reduction in the income of the average family and increasing inequality among wage earners and their families. Uneven economic and spatial development of cities have yielded unequal access to income and wealth for city residents. . . . Poverty has grown much faster in central cities than in suburban and nonmetropolitan areas with the greatest increases occurring in larger cities with large minority populations. Racial minorities are also more highly concentrated in poor neighborhoods. . . . The increasing incidence of crime, drug abuse, teenage pregnancy, school dropout rates, and other indicators of so-called underclass behavior are clearly linked to the deindustrialization, disinvestment and isolation of city neighborhoods outside the central business district (Squires 1994).

THE LOS ANGELES RIOTS: AMERICA'S WAKE-UP CALL OF THE 1990S

With 53 deaths, over 2,000 injuries and property damage exceeding $500 million, the 1992 Los Angeles (L.A.) conflagration served as a wake-up call and a reminder that the problems of urban America could not be ignored with impunity. President George Bush and his administration used the opportunity to malign the War on Poverty program's efforts to mobilize the disenfranchised minorities and economically disadvantaged in the 1960s. On May 4, 1992, Bush spokesman Marlin Fitzwater said that the failure of President Lyndon B. Johnson's Great Society anti-poverty programs of the 1960s was responsible for "many of the root problems that have resulted in inner-city difficulties" (Rovener, Duman, Kellam and Zuckman 1992).

However, the urban uprisings in several U.S. cities, which were characterized by some as efforts of disenfranchised citizens to participate in the political process, went a long way to reveal the gross deterioration of inner-city communities as well as the hopelessness of many residents. Approximately two weeks after the Los Angeles uprising, over 100,000 people marched to Washington for a Save Our Cities/Save Our Children rally. Additionally, both houses of Congress approved legislation for aid to inner-cities that included job training, unemployment benefits, emergency assistance and small business loans. However, shortly after losing the presidential election, President Bush vetoed the legislation on November 4, 1992, because, he argued, the original purpose of the bill was to provide tax benefits to help revitalize urban areas but the goal was "lost in a blizzard of special interest pleading." Therefore, the 1980s began with government efforts to dismantle citizen participation mandates, while the 1990s began with disenfranchised citizens using violence to demand a more equitable distribution of power in American society (Rovener, Duman, Kellam and Zuckman 1992).

THE MOTOR VOTER BILL AND EFFORTS TO REINVIGORATE CITIZEN PARTICIPATION

President Clinton and congressional leaders hearkened to the cries of previously disempowered residents by enacting the Motor Voter Bill on May 20, 1996 (Congressional Quarterly Almanac, 1996). The bill marked a dramatic change from the Reagan and Bush administrations by signaling federal efforts at facilitating participation among local residents. The bill requires states to provide all citizens with the opportunity to register to vote when they apply for or renew drivers' licenses. States are also required to provide mail-in registration as well as registration forms at welfare agencies. When signing the bill into law, President Clinton noted that "voting is an empty promise unless people vote and that there is no longer the excuse of the difficulty of registration" (Congressional Quarterly Almanac, 1993).

Unlike previous federal efforts to encourage non-electoral political participation, the Motor Voter legislation makes a concerted effort to mobilize voters and involve them in the electoral process. Indeed, theorists have argued that Byzantine voting procedures are a prominent cause for nonvoting among low-income and unlettered Americans (Piven and Cloward 1987). They argue that reformation of the voting registration requirements would lead to increased participation in politics and a transformation of American political parties. The Clinton administration endorsement of the Motor Voter legislation, therefore, has gone a long way to remove some of the hurdles that have prevented the electoral mobilization of some disadvantaged American citizenry.

Political scientists have noted increases in voter participation among urban residents since the enactment of the Motor Voter Bill. In a comparison of voter turnout and registration in the 1992 and 1996 presidential elections, a study has demonstrated that rates of voter registration and turnout are significantly higher in Motor Voter states than in other states (Franklin and Grier 1997).

However, the full benefits of the legislation have been stymied by the lack of policy emphasis on the contextual factors which deter or impede participation in electoral activities. In terms of domestic policy, the Clinton administration used the strategy of universalism, as endorsed by sociologist William Julius Wilson, in pursing urban goals through nonurban policy. In this way, President Clinton attempted to gain the hidden agenda of assisting poor and racial minority urban residents without alienating suburbanites. Some legislative efforts were defeated by Republican filibustering, while others like the Earned Income Tax Credit, Empowerment Zones/Enterprise Communities, and the Crime Bill had limited benefits for urban areas. The overall assessment, however, is that the foregoing policies have done little to stem the tide of uneven development, inequality, family deterioration and concentrated poverty neighborhoods which go a long way to hinder involvement in voting.

A report titled the "State of the Cities," which was issued during the June 1997 U.S. Conference of Mayors, demonstrates that America has made little progress toward addressing the problems of inequalities that continue to ravage cities. According to the report, the June 1997 unemployment rate for Americans was 4.8%, while the average for cities was 6.2%, with some local rates as high as 40%. The report also emphasized that most new jobs, even those with low pay and low skill requirements, are being created in the suburbs. Above all, the report indicated that poverty has not declined but increased since the mid-1970s, which mark the beginning of efforts to dismantle citizen participation mandates. In the 1970s, the poverty rate in inner cities was 14%. By 1995, however, it stood at 21%.[1]

Some scholars have argued that cities will continue to be plagued by gross inequalities because the current municipal arrangements have made it impossible for cities to be much more than repositories for the poor. The key to effacing the separate but equal mandate which has engulfed cities is to amalgamate cities and suburbs, which will broaden the tax base and force middle-class and impoverished residents into the same jurisdictions. This proposal is expected to insure middle-class involvement in the resolution of urban problems (Rusk 1993).

The viability of creating municipal areas without separate city/suburban boundaries is evidenced in so-called elastic cities, which have the ability to annex new suburban territories. Cities like Columbus, Ohio; San Diego, California; and Houston, Texas, for example, are perplexed by the problems of poverty, inadequate housing, and family deterioration, but the depth of problems are much less severe than so-called inelastic cities. In contrast to elastic cities, the growth of inelastic cities like Cleveland, Ohio; Detroit, Michigan; Miami, Florida; and Hartford, Connecticut, is often restricted as a result of being hemmed in by hostile suburbs. As appealing as the idea of erasing the dividing lines between inner cities and suburbia may seem, however, residents in metropolitan areas are actually engaging in participatory activity that will lead to the increased separation of racial minorities and the poor from the middle class. The next section of the chapter discusses these strategies as well as their consequences for the practice of democracy in American cities.

OUT OF SIGHT, OUT OF MIND: EFFORTS TO ESCAPE THE SCOURGE OF URBAN INEQUALITY

Unaddressed by national and municipal elected officials, low-income as well as affluent urban residents have adopted the strategy of succession as a way of coping with the overwhelming magnitude of poverty and its deleterious consequences. The warning issued by George Bernard Shaw almost 40 years ago, however, suggests that running from poverty is not effective, because one cannot hide from its consequences. This section of the chapter assesses how the strategy of secession affects the practice of democracy in American urban areas.

Such poverty as we have today in all our great cities degrades the poor, and infects with its degradation the whole neighborhood in which they live. And whatever can degrade a neighborhood can degrade a country and a continent and finally the whole civilized world, which is only a large neighborhood. Its bad effects cannot be escaped by the rich. When poverty produces outbreaks of virulent infectious disease, as it always does sooner or later, the rich catch the disease and see their children die of it. When it produces crime and violence the rich go in fear of both, and are put to a good deal of expense to protect their persons and property. When it produces bad manners and bad language children of the rich pick them up no matter how carefully they are secluded; and such seclusion as they get does them more harm than good. . . . The old notion that people can "keep themselves to themselves" and not be touched by what is happening to their neighborhoods, or even to the people who live a hundred miles off, is a most dangerous mistake. . . . though the rich end of the town can avoid living with the poor end, it cannot avoid dying with it when the plague comes, said George Bernard Shaw. (1928 as quoted in Jennings 1994)

INCORPORATION, GATED COMMUNITIES AND SPECIAL DISTRICTS: SECESSION POLITICS AMONG WEALTHY URBANITES

Many urban areas have witnessed the unabated increase of enclave communities, where affluent urban residents isolate themselves behind walls and other architectural structures that are guarded by private security patrols. These gated communities within urban as well as suburban areas represent the attempts of the affluent citizens to escape from poverty and its deleterious consequences.

While such communities are more visible during the 1990s, affluent urban residents have utilized the participatory mechanisms of government as well as the resources of wealth, commerce and social networking since the 1950s to create special districts which exclude African Americans. In a well-written and informative book on the formation of American local governments, Professor Nancy Burns convincingly demonstrates that racial effects, above and beyond the influence of economic concerns, have led to the creation of homogenous white suburbs and special districts.

However, the most profound consequences of special districts are the ways in which they influence the nature of government accountability and citizen participation (Burns 1994). In many instances, the special districts created by wealthy citizens are not accountable to other local, state or federal governments. Moreover, accountability on the part of political officials is limited by the following factors: First, since special districts are exempt from one-person, one-vote requirements, the act of living in a district does not qualify a citizen for participation, and citizens who hold property in a district but do not reside there may have the right to vote. Second, special districts are frequently not required to hold regular elections. Third, members of the governing boards of special districts may either be electorate or appointed, and the latter often do not include the opinions of citizens (Burns 1994).

Furthermore, business elements of the urban communities across the United States have also attempted to cloister themselves within the confines of gated and secured environments as an escape from the concentrated poverty neighborhoods and impoverished city residents. Urban renaissance malls in many U.S. cities are located in downtown areas, but are architecturally enclosed and distinct from the surrounding impoverished areas (Judd and Swanstrom, forthcoming). Even downtown business offices, which primarily house white-collar office workers, are demarcated from surrounding areas. Not only is the turf of downtown business communities secured by internal security forces, but it is demarcated by physical barriers including convention centers, freeway ramps, and sports stadiums. For many white-collar workers, the physical walls and architectural designs of the downtown business sector make it possible to drive into secured parking garages and then enter a city-within-a-city where they can eat, shop and work and play (Judd and Swanstrom, forthcoming). These enclave residential and business communities have provided more-affluent urban residents with a false sense of security and a limited conception of the racial, spatial, class and familial inequalities that exist in urban America.

While it is certainly rational for urban residents to seclude themselves from the perils of poverty and its associated consequences, there is no escape from the ultimate consequences of urban inequalities, especially the proliferation of concentrated poverty neighborhoods and single-parent households. As the foregoing quotation by George Bernard Shaw indicates, the affluent may run, but they cannot hide from the consequences of poverty and urban inequalities. The walls of affluent residents and business communities will not always prevail against the increasing frustrations among white and black inner-city residents who cannot adequately feed, clothe or house their families because of uneven economic development. Inequalities in educational resources—which result from inadequate municipal imperatives that provide abatements to wealthy corporations but reductions in school budgets—render many inner-city high school graduates incapable of finding decent jobs. This unfortunate situation will eventually debilitate the whole of American society by polluting its workforce and creating a permanently dependent class. Moreover, the scourges of AIDS and, most recently, tuberculosis that result from uneven economic development and inadequate health facilities will taint the American blood supply and infect the poor and the affluent alike.

While the effects of crime, limited employment opportunities and racial conflict have traversed the walls of many suburban communities across the United States, the most visible affect of the ability of affluent urban residents to exclude racial minorities and the poor is the exacerbation of the existing inequalities. Cities and inner-ring suburbs are increasingly strapped for money to meet the pressing needs of poorer and more heavily black and Hispanic populations. Meanwhile, wealthier outer-ring suburbs, middle class and largely white, enjoy most of the job growth and regional success.

As a result of the widening gaps between the haves and the have-nots, there have been attempts on the part of racial minorities to secede from urban governments and form their own communities and school districts. Unlike the successful efforts of affluent whites to create special districts and suburban communities which exclude the poor and racial minorities, many of the secession attempts on the part of the poor and racial minorities have been unsuccessful. However, they are important for two reasons. First, the attempts to secede are an implicit declaration of the failure of racial integration for many impoverished racial minorities. Second, these attempts underscore the racism, socio-economic discrimination and neglect that reverberate in many inner-city communities. The secession attempts in Boston, Massachusetts, an inelastic city that is hemmed in by suburbs, are instructive in this regard.

THE MANDELA REFERENDUM: THE MOVEMENT FOR URBAN NATIONALISM

In 1986, disenchanted residents of Boston, Massachusetts, began a movement known as the Mandela Referendum, named after the then imprisoned South African leader, President Nelson Mandela. According to movement organizers, the Mandela Referendum was an attempt by people at the grass-roots level to circumvent the formal mechanisms of citizen participation and take control of their own affairs. The proposal included the act of secession from the city of Boston and reincorporation as the city of Mandela. The proposed city was to be comprised of 60% black, 25% white and 15% Asian and Latino citizens, making it one of the most racially-cum-ethnically diverse communities in the city. Similar to the logic of the Johnson administration maximum feasible participation, proponents of the Mandela incorporation argued that the first step to solving economic problems of poor communities in Boston and other metropolitan areas was for poor blacks to become actively involved in the political process. They argued further that political control of the policy-making agenda, as evinced by the ability of black political leaders to devise and implement ameliorative policies, would go a long way to close the gaps of racial and socio-economic class disparities between blacks and whites.

Proponents of the Mandela Referendum argued that attempts by blacks to effect positive policy change had resulted in only ephemeral policy concessions. Supporters of the referendum utilized the intransigence of residential and school segregation—which was the root cause of economic disparities—as evidence of the limited impact of black elected officials. They argued that blacks were already crippled by the uneven development within the city as well as development disparities between inner-city and suburban areas. Proponents of the referendum also underscored the disfranchisement from the political decision-making in Boston. They maintained that the incorporation of Mandela would provide blacks with not only an opportunity for participation but also the autonomy needed to provide positive benefits for the black community.

The grievances enumerated by proponents of Mandela were not contrived but real. The commercial areas of black neighborhoods were filled with boarded-up apartment buildings, trash-filled vacant lots, liquor stores and check cashing offices. Gentrification and the concomitant increase in housing and land values have displaced many of the areas' black residents. In a three-year span of time, the average increase of one-bedroom-apartment rentals was $300, while homes that used to sell for $60,000 increased by 300% over three years (House 1988). While the accelerating real estate values have been attributed to Boston's high-tech economy, many blacks have suffered from housing displacement and the lack of skills which precludes them from the high-tech job market (House 1988).

The economic indicators of the predominantly black neighborhoods that were scheduled to comprise Mandela are also troubling. At the time of the referendum, the unemployment rate was 20%. Additionally, over 30% of the families lived below the poverty line, and the neighborhood schools have experienced severe crises, with some drop-out rates approaching 50% (House 1988).

Black as well as poor white Bostonians have also complained of chronic inaccessibility to the policy-making process and political leaders. Officials of the local National Association for the Advancement of Colored People (NAACP) filed a lawsuit against Mayor Flynn and the Boston Housing Authority in 1988 after requests for a meeting about public housing desegregation were ignored for eight months (Hernandez and Marantz 1989). Other community groups have also been rebuffed by Mayor Flynn and other Boston political officials. After attempts to meet with him failed, the Association of Community Organizations for Reform (ACORN) staged a sit-in, but their efforts to meet with him were not heeded (Hernandez and Marantz 1989). ACORN vice-president aptly summed up the sentiments of many disenfranchised Bostonians with the following statement: "He has a preference in who he responds to. . . . I would say his access is not open or closed but limited to certain people" (Hernandez and Marantz 1989).

Additionally, proponents of the Mandela Referendum have argued that the racial overtones of recent public scandals augur well for secession. They cited the second-mortgage scandal in which unscrupulous lenders and contractors preyed on minority homeowners with impunity from city officials; the abolition of an elected school committee, with four black members, which leaves black parents with little access to and influence on the educational system; the absence of a single citywide black official; and the Stuart murder case in which the police focused concerted attention on the black community only to realize that the so-called grieving husband was actually the perpetrator.

Opponents of the referendum agreed that black Bostonians had persistently been plagued by the consequences of racism and some access problems, but they seriously questioned the extent to which the incorporation of Mandela would provide the organizational mechanisms and resources to effectively reduce income and service disparities (Haggard-Gilson 1995). After all, Mandela would have to contend with reducing service disparities among citizens who were already handicapped by the problems of persistent discrimination. Consequently, Mandela officials would need a large arsenal of financial and social service resources to rectify the problems and establish a sound financial footing.

As tempting as the notion of incorporation seemed, opponents of Mandela were not adequately convinced that the city of Mandela—as conceived by referendum proponents—could survive and thrive economically. The structural inequities that have persisted for decades would not cease to exist because of the act of secession and incorporation. Opponents argued that Mandela would be a poor city that would ultimately be dependent on state funds. Advocates acknowledged the difficulties but hastily added that the city of Mandela would be fiscally solvent because of its prime location and the growth of the area's economy.

Five factors helped to defeat the Mandela Referendum, which was part of the 1986 and 1988 ballot. First, was Mayor Flynn's crafty utilization of the media. Second, the mayor made frequent appearances in the black community, especially during voting time. Third, Mayor Flynn was able to garner and adequately utilize the support of many of Boston's black ministers. Fourth, his advocacy of affordable housing and jobs as well as job training went a long way to provide the appearances of concrete as well as tangible success (Overbea 1986). The fifth and final factor is the low rate of black voter participation, which limited the number of positive votes for the Referendum. Additionally, the mayor emphasized development projects in the Boston community, which helped to boost his credibility in the black community. The Mandela Referendum was voted on and defeated in 1986 and 1988 as a result of concerns about the economic viability of the proposed city of Mandela.

While the Mandela Referendum was not successful in achieving its goal of incorporation, many black and white officials contended that it shed light on the black community's problem and got people involved. Moreover, the efforts for secession, especially on the part of the urban poor, are not limited to the city of Boston. Indeed, the currently bankrupt city of East Palo Alto, a black community in northern California, adopted a strategy of secession or urban nationalism without the necessary economic resources. The lack of resources has ironically led to a state of hyper-dependence as residents of this predominantly black community are forced to depend on surrounding counties, and the State of California for aid. Unbowed by these unsuccessful experiments in urban nationalism as well as the failure of the 1986 and 1988 Mandela Referendum, residents in the New York boroughs of Staten Island and Queens have expressed similar frustration with the status quo of urban politics and have forged ahead to begin movements for secession.

Overall, the concept of secession is a troubling one for urban communities and the country as we approach the twenty-first century. Thirty years after the Civil Rights movement, American cities continue to be embroiled in deep racial and class tensions. While America is often regarded by its own citizens as well as others as the great experiment in democracy, many residents of inner-city communities have not been accorded an equal opportunity to participate in either democratic capitalism or democracy in general. As a result of impediments at both the neighborhood and family levels, which are, in some measure, the result of gross structural inequalities, many urban residents are not part of the social, economic and political processes affecting them. Indeed, John Stuart Mill convincingly argued that "the rights and interests of every or any person are only secure from being disregarded, when the person interested is himself able, and habitually disposed, to stand up for them" (Nagel 1987). This sentiment was echoed by Professor James Jennings, an expert on urban poverty and political activism:

> The social and economic problems of Blacks in America will not be overcome until Blacks control institutions of power such as schools, banks, social agencies, health organizations and the like. It is the lack of power which allows the continuing economic and cultural exploitation of Black people. Black communities must be able to develop the wherewithal to stop or veto economic or educational processes which are imposed or are not clear about direct benefits to community residents. The political ability to stop things from occurring is not a panacea, but it is a necessary first step. (Jennings 1992a)

The findings of this study have suggested that the impediments of national policy and the current inner-city social context must be removed by a renewed emphasis on eliminating the political disenfranchisement and the social-cum-economic inequalities that prevent white as well as black impoverished inner-city residents from loudly proclaiming their political interests and boldly exercising their political rights.

NOTE

1. *The Economist*, June 28, 1997, p. 29.

Questionnaire

Neighborhood Services:

Now I'd like to begin by finding out how satisfied you are with some of the services in your neighborhood. What about the quality of neighborhood shopping, that is grocery stores or drug stores? Are you very dissatisfied, dissatisfied, satisfied, or very satisfied?

What about city services like trash collection? Are you very dissatisfied, dissatisfied, satisfied or very satisfied?

Neighborhood Criminal Activity:

Now, I am going to read a list of problems that exist in some neighborhoods. First, theft or burglary. Is it not a problem at all, somewhat of a problem or a big problem?

Illegal drug activity. Is it not a problem at all, somewhat of a problem or a big problem?

How about personal safety when walking around the neighborhood? Is it not a problem at all, somewhat of a problem or a big problem?

Social Isolation:

When you think of the kind of people that you would like the children in your neighborhood to be like, do these upwardly mobile individuals live in your neighborhood or somewhere else?

Do most of your friends live in your neighborhood or somewhere else?

We are interested in the kinds of neighborhood, civic and religious organizations you belong to. As I read the list please tell me whether anyone in your household belongs to the organization. A neighborhood improvement association. Is it you, someone else in the household or both? A labor union? Is it you, someone else in the household or both? A fraternal lodge, fraternity or sorority? Is it you, someone else in your household or both? A parent-teachers' organization? Is it you, someone else in your household or both? A neighborhood crime patrol? Is it you, someone else in the household or both? A business association? Is it you, someone else in the household or both?

Religious Involvement:

Now, on to a different subject. Is your religious preference Protestant, Catholic, Jewish, Islamic, some other religion or no religion?

How often do you attend religious services? Never, less than once a year, about once or twice a year, several times a year, once a month, two to three times a month, nearly every week, every week or more than once a week.

Interest in Political Affairs:

We are interested in what people think and feel about government and politics. How interested are you in national/local politics? Are you very interested, somewhat interested, not too interested, not interested at all?

Political Communication:

How interested in national politics are most of the people you know? Would you say very interested, somewhat interested, not too interested, not interested at all? How about national politics? Are most of the people you know very interested, somewhat interested, not too interested, not interested at all?

How often do you discuss local politics? Would you say very often, somewhat, not too often or never? How about national politics? Do you discuss it very often, somewhat, not too often or never?

Here is a list of people that one might discuss politics with, family members, church members, people at work and people in the neighborhood. Which of these people do you discuss politics with?

Party Identification:

Now, I'd like to talk to you about political parties. Generally speaking, do you usually think of yourself as a Republican, Democrat, Independent or what?

Political Efficacy:

Do you think the public has control over what politicians do in office?

Civil Disobedience:

There are many ways for people to show their disagreement with government actions. I am going to describe three such ways. I would like to know which ones you approve of as ways of showing dissatisfaction with government, and which ones you disapprove of. How about refusing to obey a law which you think is unfair, if the person feels so strongly about it that he is willing to go to jail rather than obey the law? Would you approve or disapprove of a person doing that?

Suppose other forms of participation like voting, petitioning and campaigning have failed and the person decides to try to stop the government from going about its usual activities with sit-ins, demonstrations and things like that. Would you approve or disapprove? Do you think that people are justified in rioting when other methods have failed?

Electoral Activities:

In talking about politics, we find that some people are not registered to vote for a number of reasons. Are you currently registered to vote? Now, thinking about presidential elections since you were old enough to vote, have you always voted, sometimes voted or hardly ever voted in presidential elections? Thinking about local elections in Columbus since you were eligible to vote, have you always voted or hardly ever voted in local elections?

Non-electoral Activities:

Now, I am going to read a list of political activities that people sometimes participate in. In the last four years, have you participated in a protest march, boycott or rally?

How about signing a petition to get someone's name on a ballot or in support of an issue? Never, once, more than once?

In the last four years, how often have you attended a community meeting to get information on a candidate or issue? Was it never, once or more than once?

In the last four years, how often have you contacted a public official to solve a problem or get information about an issue? Would you say never, once or more than once?

In the last four years, have you worked with others to solve community problems? Would you say never, once or more than once?

Economic Marginalization:

Is your home paid for, are you buying it, or do you rent?

Do you or does anyone in your household own a car or truck?

Family Context:

The family context variable measures the structure of the household. It is comprised of responses from the following questions: In our surveys, we have found that the number of people in a household varies. Some people live alone, while others are married. Some have children, while others do not. How about you? Are you currently married, living with a partner, widowed, divorced, separated or never married? Do you have any children? How many of these children are between the ages of six and 18?

Neighborhood Context:

During the computer assisted telephone interview, survey interviewers confirmed the current addresses of respondents to insure that they were in the targeted census tract and neighborhood association boundaries. Once the survey was completed, the neighborhood context variable was operationalized as follows: Individuals who resided in neighborhoods where the poverty level was 40% or above were coded as concentrated poverty residents, while those who lived in neighborhoods with a poverty rate of 20% or below were coded as low poverty neighborhood residents.

Income:

We'd like a general range of your family income. That is, of the total income of all members of your family living with you for 1992 before taxes. This figure should include salaries, wages, pensions, dividends, interests and all other income. We are not asking for exact numbers. Was it under $5,000 or over $5,000 (this question is repeated for 5,000 increments until 50,000).

Education:

Now, we'd like to ask some questions about you. In studies like these, we often compare the ideas of men and women, young and old people, and people of different economic and educational backgrounds. So, we need to know about you. Again, all of your answers are strictly confidential. How many years of school have you completed?

Gender:

Recorded by interviewer as either male or female.

Religious Involvement:

How often do clergy in your church discuss political issues from the pulpit—frequently, sometimes, rarely or never?

Recruitment:

Did anyone encourage you to participate in (interviewer inserted the name of the activity that respondent reported participating in)? Was it someone at home, work, church or in your neighborhood?

The responses were tallied and combined into a scale which measured the number of times individuals were encouraged (mobilized or recruited) to participate in non-electoral activities.

Political Interest:

The political interest scale[1] is the sum of answers to the following questions about local and national interest: Thinking about local politics, how interested are you in local community politics and issues? Would you say very interested, somewhat interested, slightly interested or not at all interested? How interested are you in national politics and national affairs? (The "very interested" response was coded as 4 and "not at all" response was coded as 1. The additive scale ranges from 2 to 8. The two items were highly correlated with a Pearson correlation of .686.)

Electoral Participation:

The electoral participation variable was constructed by combining the responses for the questions on national and local elections.[2] The responses include the following: In talking with people about politics, we often find that some people are not registered to vote for a number of reasons. Are you currently registered to vote? Now, thinking about the presidential elections since you were old enough to vote, have you always voted, sometimes voted or hardly ever voted in presidential elections? Thinking about local elections in Columbus, Ohio, since you were eligible to vote, have you always voted, sometimes voted or hardly ever voted in local elections? (Each question was given a value of 0 through 4 (0=hardly ever voted, 4 always voted). The scale runs from 0 to 8, with a Pearson correlation of .803.)

Organizational Membership:

We are interested in the kinds of neighborhood, civic and religious organizations you belong to. As I read the list, please tell me whether anyone in your household belongs to the organization.

The list of possible responses included (0) nobody; (1) respondent only; (2) someone else in household; (3) respondent and other household members. The organizational membership scale was constructed by adding the number of organizations that the respondent belongs to. The scale ranged from 0 to 6, including the following organizations (neighborhood improvement association; neighborhood business association; neighborhood crime patrol; labor union; a fraternity, lodge or sorority; a parent teacher organization; the NAACP).

NOTES

1. A similar scale was utilized by Verba, Schlozman and Brady in their critically acclaimed 1995 study, *Voice and Equality*.

2. A similar voting scale was utilized by Verba, Schlozman and Brady in their critically acclaimed 1995 study of political participation, *Voice and Equality*.

Methodological Appendix

SPSS and STATA software packages were utilized to perform the contingency table and path analyses. The regression analysis for this study was conducted in two distinct phases. First, successive, reduced form equations are used to decompose the total effects into their direct and indirect effects. Based on a scheme developed by Alwin and Hauser, this computation of reduced form equations begins with a model which contains only exogenous variables in the system, then successively adds the variables or sets of variables that intervene, effectively proceeding in sequence from cause to effect until the intervening variables are exhausted. This generates all of the information required to decompose the total effects into their various mediated and un-mediated parts (Asher 1990).

Second, analysis of co-variance (ANACOVA) was utilized to determine whether the effects of independent variables differ significantly by race. Specifically, the ANACOVA process adopted for this study used reverse dummy variable coding, in which two dummy variables for race are interacted with each independent variable, and two parallel OLS or LOGIT (for the social isolation variable) equations are estimated for each model. Thus, one set of OLS or LOGIT equations includes the black dummy variable, the interaction variables between black and all independent variables, and the original independent variables. The interaction term coefficients, from these equations, indicate how much the independent variables affect blacks differently from whites. The interaction term t-values indicate whether these racial differences are statistically significant. Reversing this analysis provides the models' main effects coefficients for blacks. Thus, a second set of OLS and LOGIT equations is computed including the white dummy variable, the interactions between white and all independent variables, and the original independent variables. The main effects variables in these equations provide the independent variables' coefficients and t-values for blacks. In both cases, the black and white coefficients provide the effect of race beyond the effects of all other independent variables. The final results are equivalent to running the separate OLS and LOGIT equations for blacks and whites separately but with tests for racial differences. In fact, separate OLS and LOGIT equations were run to obtain separately adjusted r-square statistics and probability values for blacks and whites.

Bibliography

Aberbach, Joel D. 1969. "Alienation and Political Behavior." *American Political Science Review*. 63:76–89.

Abramowitz, Mimi.1991. "Putting an End to Doublespeak About Race, Gender and Poverty." *Social Work*. 36(5):383

———. 1992. "The New Paternalism." *The Nation*. 255:368–371.

Abramson, Paul R. 1983. *Political Attitudes in America*. San Francisco: W.H. Freeman and Company.

Acs, Gregory. 1996. "The Impact of Welfare on Young Mothers' Subsequent Childbearing Decisions." *Journal of Human Resources*. 31(4):898–916.

Aldrich, John H. 1993. "Rational Choice and Turnout." *American Journal of Political Science*. 37:246–247.

Alex-Assensoh, Yvette. 1995. "Myths About Race and the Urban Underclass: Concentrated Poverty and Underclass Behaviors." *Urban Affairs Review*. 31(1):3–19.

Almond, Gabriel A. and Sidney Verba. 1965. *The Civic Culture*. Princeton: Princeton University Press.

Alston, Jon, and Imogene Dean. 1972. "Socioeconomic Factors Associated with Attitudes Toward Welfare Participants and the Causes of Poverty." *Social Science Review*. 46:13–23.

Anderson, Elijah. 1989. "Sex Codes and Family Life Among Poor Inner-City Fathers." *The Annals*. 501:59–78.

———. 1991. "Neighborhood Effects on Teenage Pregnancy," *The Urban Underclass*, Christopher Jencks and Paul Peterson, editors. Washington:The Brookings Institution.

Anderson, Kristi, and Elizabeth Cook. 1985. "Women, Work and Political Attitudes." *American Journal of Political Science*. 29:606–25.

Audrey, Saundra. 1994. "The Political Behavior of Black Women: Contextual, Structural, and Psychological Factors," *Black Politics and Black Political Behavior*, Hanes Walton, Jr., editor. Westport: Praeger.

Asher, Herbert B. 1990. *Causal Modeling*. Newbury Park: Sage Publications.

Auclair, Philip. 1984. "Public Attitudes Toward Social Welfare Expenditures." *Social Work*. 29:139–44.

Auletta, Ken. 1982. *The Underclass*. New York: Vintage.

Bane, Mary Jo, and David T. Ellwood. 1994. *Welfare Realities: From Rhetoric to Reform*. Cambridge: Harvard University Press.

Banfield, Edward. 1970. *The Unheavenly City*. Boston: Little, Brown.

Barnes, Samuel H., et al. 1979. *Political Action: Mass Participation in Five Western Democracies*. Beverly Hills: Sage.

Baxter, Sandra and Marjorie Lansing. 1983. *Women and Politics: The Visible Majority*. Ann Arbor: University of Michigan Press.

Beck, Paul. 1974. "A Socialization Theory of Partisan Realignment," *The Politics of Future Citizens*, Richard G. Niemi, editor. San Francisco: Jossey-Bass.

———. 1976. "A Socialization Theory of Partisan Realignment," *Controversies in American Voting Behavior*, Richard G. Niemi and Herbert F. Weisberg, editors. San Francisco: Freeman.

———. 1991. "Voters Intermediation Environments in the 1988 Presidential Contest." *Public Opinion Quarterly*. 55:371–95.

———, and M. Kent Jennings. 1975. "Parents as Middlepersons in Political Socialization." *Journal of Politics*. 37:83–107.

———, and Kent Jennings.1992. "Family Traditions, Political Periods and the Development of Partisan Orientation." *Journal of Politics*. 53:742–763.

Berry, Jeffrey, Kent Portney and Ken Thomson. 1991. "The Political Behavior of Poor People," *The Urban Underclass*. Washington: The Brookings Institution.

———. 1993. *The Rebirth of Urban Democracy*. Washington, D.C.: The Brookings Institution.

Blank, Rebecca. "Analyzing the Length of Welfare Spells." *Journal of Public Economics*. 39:245–273.

Bobo, Lawrence, and Franklin Gilliam. 1990. "Race, Socioeconomic Status, and Black Empowerment." *American Political Science Review*. 84:377–94.

Bordieu, Pierre. 1986. "The Forms of Capital," *Handbook of Theory and Research for the Sociology of Education*, J.G. Richardson, editor. New York: Greenwood Press.

Braddock, J.H. and J.M. McPartland. 1987. "How Minorities Continue to Be Excluded from Equal Employment Opportunities: Research on Labor Market and Institutional Barriers." *Journal of Social Issues.* 43:5–39.

Brady, Henry, Sidney Verba and Kay Schlozman. 1995. "Beyond SES: A Resource Model of Political Participation." *American Political Science Review.* 89(2):271–294.

Brody, Richard. 1978. "The Puzzle of Political Participation in America." *The New American Political System,* Anthony King, editor. Washington, D.C.: American Enterprise Institute.

Burns, Nancy. 1994. *The Formation of American Local Government.* New York: Oxford University Press.

Button, James. 1989. *Blacks and Social Change.* Princeton: Princeton University Press.

Campbell, Angus, Phillip E. Converse, Warren E. Miller, and Donald E. Stokes. 1960. *The American Voter.* Chicago: University of Chicago Press.

———, Gerald Gurin, and Warren E. Miller. 1954. *The Voter Decides.* Evanston: Row, Peterson and Co.

Carmines, Edward, and James Stimson. 1989. *Issue Evolution: Race and the Transformation of American Politics.* Princeton: Princeton University Press.

Clark, Cal, and Janet Clark. 1986. "Models of Gender and Political Participation in the United States." *Women and Politics.* 6:5–25.

Cohen, Cathy, and Michael Dawson. 1993. "Neighborhood Poverty and African American Politics." *American Political Science Review.* 87(2):286–302.

Congressional Quarterly Almanac. 1993. Washington, D.C.: Congressional Quarterly News Features.

Conway, Margaret. 1991. *Political Participation in the United States.* Washington, D.C.: Congressional Quarterly Press.

Cook, Fay, and Edith Barrett. 1992. *Support for the American Welfare State.* New York: Columbia University Press.

Corcoran, Mary, et al. 1985. "Myth and Reality: The Causes and Persistence of Poverty." *Journal of Policy Analysis and Management.* 4:516–536.

Cott, Nancy F. 1990. "Across the Great Divide: Women in Politics Before and After 1920," In *Women and Political Change*, Patricia Gurin and Louise A. Tilly, editors. New York: Sage.

Crane, Jonathan. 1991. "Effects of Neighborhood on Dropping out of School and Teenage Childbearing," *The Urban Underclass,* Christopher Jencks and Paul Peterson, editors. Washington, D.C.: Brookings Institution.

Crenson, Matthew. 1983. *Neighborhood Politics*. Cambridge: Harvard University Press.

Daft, Betty. 1979. "The Old Neighborhoods." *Columbus Dispatch Magazine*. 35:14–15.

Dahl, Robert A. 1961. *Who Governs? Democracy and Power in an American City*. New Haven: Yale University Press.

Danziger, Sheldon, and Peter Gottschalk. 1995. *America Unequal*. New York and Cambridge: Russell Sage Foundation and Harvard University Press.

Dawson, Michael. 1994. *Behind The Mule: Race and Class in African-American Politics*. Princeton: Princeton University Press.

Easton, David. 1965. *A Framework for Political Analysis*. New York: Prentice-Hall.

Eggers, Mitchell, and Douglass Massey. 1992. " A Longitudinal Analysis of Urban Poverty: Blacks in U.S. Metropolitan Areas Between 1970 and 1980." *Social Science Research*. 21:175–203.

———. 1991. "The Structural Determinants of Urban Poverty: A Comparison of Whites, Blacks and Hispanics." *Social Science Research*. 20:217–225.

Elkin, Stephen. 1987. *City And Regime in the American Republic*. Chicago: University of Chicago Press.

Ellison, Ralph. 1952. *Invisible Man*. New York: Random House.

Ellwood, David T., and Lawrence H. Summers. 1986. "Poverty in America: Is Welfare the Answer or Is It the Problem?" In *Fighting Poverty: What Works and What Doesn't*, Sheldon Danziger and David Weinberg, editors. Cambridge: Harvard University Press.

Erickson, Bonnie H., and T.A. Nosanchuk. 1990. "How an Apolitical Association Politicizes." *Canadian Review of Sociology and Anthropology*. 27:206–219.

Erie, Steven P. 1988. *Rainbow's End*. Berkeley: University of California Press.

Fainstein Norman I. and Susan Fainstein.1974. *Urban Political Movements: The Search for Power by Minority Groups in American Cities*. Englewood Cliffs, NJ: Prentice-Hall.

Feagin, Joe R. 1975. *Subordinating the Poor: Welfare and American Beliefs*. Englewood Cliffs, NJ: Prentice-Hall.

———. 1991. "The Continuing Significance of Race: Antiblack Discrimination in Public Places." *American Sociological Review*. 56:101–116.

Fenno, Richard, Jr. 1978. *Homestyle: House Members in Their Districts*. Boston: Little, Brown and Co.

Fernandez, Roberto and David Harris. 1992. "Social Isolation and the Underclass," *Drugs, Crime and Social Isolation: Barriers to Urban*

Opportunity, Adele V. Harrell and George E. Peterson, editors. Washington, D.C.: Urban Institute Press.

Finifter, Ada W. 1974. "The Friendship Group as a Protective Environment for Political Deviants." *American Political Science Review.* 68(June): 607–625.

Franklin, Daniel P. and Eric E. Grier. 1997. "Effects of Motor Voter Legislation." *American Politics Quarterly.* 25(1):104–117.

Frazier,Franklin E. 1974. *The Negro Church in America.* New York: Schocken Books.

Freeman, Richard B. 1991. "Employment and Earnings of Disadvantaged Young Men in a Labor Shortage Economy," *The Urban Underclass.* Washington, D.C.: Brookings Institution.

Gallagher, John. 1996. *Perfect Enemies: The Religious Right, the Gay Movement and the Politics of the 1990s.* New York: Crown Publishers.

Giddings, Paula. 1984. *When and Where I Enter: The Impact of Black Women on Race and Sex in America.* New York: Morrow.

Gilder, George. 1981. *Wealth and Poverty.* New York: Basic Books.

Giles, Michael. 1977. "Percent Black and Racial Hostility: An Old Assumption Reexamined." *Social Science Quarterly.* 58:412–417.

———, and Marilyn K. Dantico. 1982. "Political Participation and Neighborhood Social Context Revisited." *American Journal of Political Science.* 26:144–150.

———, and Kaenan Hertz. 1994. "Racial Threat and Partisan Identification." *American Political Science Review.* 88(2):317–326.

———, and Melanie Buckner. 1993. "David Duke and Black Threat: An Old Hypothesis Revisited." *Journal of Politics.* 55(3):702–713.

———, Gerald Wright and Marilyn Dantico. 1981. "Social Status and Political Behavior: The Impact of Residential Context." *Social Science Quarterly.* 62:453–460.

Gilliam, Frank D. Jr., and Kenny Whitby. 1989. "Race, Class and Attitudes Toward Social Welfare Spending: An Ethclass Interpretation." *Social Science Quarterly.* 62:453–460.

Green, Richard R. 1990. "Poverty, Concentration Measures and the Urban Underclass." *Economic Geography.* 67(3):240–252.

———. 1991. "Poverty Area Diffusion: The Depopulation Hypothesis Examined." *Urban Geography.* 12:526–541.

Greenstone, David J. 1991. "Culture, Rationality and the Underclass," *The Urban Underclass,* Christopher Jencks and Paul Peterson, editors. Washington, D.C.: The Brookings Institution.

Gutterbock, Thomas M., and Bruce London. 1983. "Race, Political Orientation and Participation: An Empirical Test of Four Competing Theories." *American Sociological Review*. 48:439–453.

Haggard-Gilson, Nancy. 1995. "Boston's Mandela Referendum: Urban Nationalism and Economic Dependence." *National Political Science Review*. 5:197–214.

Handlin, Oscar.1973. *The Uprooted*. Boston: Little, Brown and Company.

Harrell, Adele V., and George Peterson. 1992. *Drugs, Crime and Social Isolation: Barriers to Urban Opportunity*. Washington, D.C.: Urban Institute Press.

Harris, Frederick C. 1994. "Something Within: Religion as a Mobilizer of African-American Political Activism." *Journal of Politics*. 56(1):42–68.

Harris, Kathleen Mullen. 1991. "Teenage Mothers and Welfare Dependence: Working off Welfare." *Journal of Family Issues*. 12(4):492–27.

———. 1993. "Work and Welfare Among Single Mothers in Poverty." *American Journal of Sociology*. 99:317–52.

Harrison, Lawrence E. 1992. *Who Prospers? How Cultural Values Shape Economic and Political Success*. New York: Basic Books.

Henry, Charles P. 1992. "Understanding the Role of the Underclass: The Role of Culture and Economic Progress," *Race, Politics, and Economic Development: Community Perspectives*, James Jennings, editor. London: Verso Press.

Hernandez, Peggy and Steven Marantz. 1989. "Flynn Can Be a Hard Mayor to Reach, Some Say." *The Boston Globe*. April 17, p. 21.

Hochschild, Jennifer. 1989. "Equal Opportunity and the Estranged Poor." *The Annals* 501:143–155.

House, Roger. November 7, 1988. "Mandela Referendum: Blacks in Boston Seek to Secede," *The Nation*. 247 (13):452.

Huckfeldt, Robert. 1979. "Political Participation and Neighborhood Social Context." *American Journal of Political Science*. 23:579–92.

———. 1983. "The Social Context of Ethnic Loyalties." *American Politics Quarterly*. 11:91–124.

———. 1986. *Politics in Context: Assimilation and Conflict in Urban Neighborhoods*. New York: Agathon.

———, and Carol Kohfeld. 1989. *Race and the Decline of Class in American Politics*. Urbana: University of Illinois Press.

———, Eric Plutzer, and John Sprague. 1993. "Alternative Contexts of Political Behavior: Churches, Neighborhoods, and Individuals." *Journal of Politics*. 55:365–381.

————, and John Sprague. 1987. "Networks in Context: The Social Flow of Political Information." *American Political Science Review.* 81:1197–1216.

————. 1988. "Choice, Social Structure and Political Information: The Informational Coercion of Minorities." *American Journal of Political Science.* 32(2):467–482.

————. 1991. "Discussant Effects on Vote Choice: Intimacy, Structure, and Interdependence." *Journal of Politics.* 53:112–58.

————. 1993. "Citizens, Contexts and Politics." *Political Science: The State of the Discipline II,* Ada Finifter, editor. Washington, D.C.: American Political Science Association.

————. 1995. *Citizens, Politics and Social Communication.* New York: Cambridge University Press.

Huges, Mark Allan. 1989. "Misspeaking Truth to Power: A Geographical Perspective on the 'Underclass' Fallacy." *Economic Geography.* 65:187–207.

Jargowsky, Paul A. and Mary Jo Bane. 1991. "Ghetto Poverty in the United States," *The Urban Underclass*, Christopher Jencks and Paul E. Peterson, editors. Washington, D.C.: Brookings Institution.

Jencks, Christopher. 1991. "Is the American Underclass Growing?" *The Urban Underclass*, Christopher Jencks and Paul Peterson, editors. Washington, D.C.: Brookings Institution.

————, and Paul Peterson, editors. 1991. *The Urban Underclass.* Washington, D.C.: Brookings Institution.

Jennings, James. 1992a. *The Politics of Black Empowerment.* Detroit: Wayne State University Press.

————. 1992b. *Race, Politics and Economic Development.* New York: Verso Publishing Company.

————.1994. *Understanding the Nature of Poverty in Urban America.* Westport: Praeger.

Jennings M. Kent, and Richard Niemi. 1968. "The Transmission of Political Values from Parent to Child." *American Political Science Review.* 62:169–84.

————. 1974. *The Political Character of Adolescence.* Princeton: Princeton University Press.

————. 1981. *Generations and Politics: A Panel Study of Young Adults and Their Parents.* Princeton: Princeton University Press.

Johnson, James H., Jr., Elisa Jayne Bienenstock, and Jennifer A. Stoloff. 1995. "An Empirical Test of the Cultural Capital Hypothesis," *Review of Black Political Economy.*

————, and Melvin Oliver. 1991. "Modeling Urban Underclass Behavior: Theoretical Considerations," UCLA Center for the Study of Urban Poverty Occassional Working Paper Series, Volume 1 (3):1–15.

————, Melvin Oliver and Lawrence Bobo, 1994. "Unraveling the Paradox of Deepening Urban Inequality: Theoretical Underpinnings and Research Design of a Multi-city Study." *Urban Geography*. 15: 77–89.

Jones, Mack H. 1992. "The Blacks Underclass as Systemic Phenomenon," *Race, Politics and Economic Development: Community Perspectives*, James Jennings, editor. New York: Verso.

Judd, Dennis. 1988. *The Politics of American Cities*. Boston: Scott, Foresman/Little, Brown College Division.

————, and Todd Swanstrom. 1994. *City Politics*. New York: HarperCollins.

————, and Todd Swanstrom. *City Politics*. New York: HarperCollins (forthcoming).

————, and Paul Kantor. *Enduring Tensions In Urban Politics*. New York: Macmillan Publishing Company. 1992.

Kasarda, John. 1985. "Urban Change and Minority Opportunities," *The New Urban Reality*, Paul Peterson, editor. Washington, D.C.: Brookings Institution.

————. 1989. "Urban Industrial Transition and the Underclass." *The Annals*. 501(22):26–47.

————. 1992. "Urban Employment Change and Minority Skills Mismatch," *Enduring Tensions in Urban Politics*, Dennis Judd and Paul Kantor, editors. New York: Macmillan Publishing Company.

Kasnick, Phillip. 1993. "The Real Jobs Problem." *Wall Street Journal*, November 26, A8.

Katz, Michael B. 1993. "Reframing the 'Underclass' Debate," *The Underclass Debate: Views from History*. Princeton: Princeton University Press.

Key, Vladimir O. 1949. *Southern Politics in State and Nation*. New York: Vintage Books.

Kirschenman, Joleen, and Kathryn Neckerman. 1991. "We'd Love to Hire Them, But . . . : The Meaning of Race for Employers," *The Urban Underclass*, Christopher Jencks and Paul Peterson, editors. Washington, D.C.: Brookings Institution.

Knoke, David. 1990. *Organizing for Collective Action: The Political Economies of Associations*. Hawthorne, NY: Aldine deGruyter.

Kohfeld, Carol and John Sprague. 1988. "Urban Unemployment Drives Urban Crime." *Urban Affairs Quarterly*. 24(2):215–241.

Kotler, Milton. 1969. *Neighborhood Government: The Local Foundations of Political Life*. Indianapolis: Bobbs-Merrill.

Kotlowitz, Alex.1991. *There Are No Children Here*. New York: Doubleday.

Kuo, Wen. 1977. "Black Political Participation: A Reconsideration." *Journal of Politics*. 25:312–323.

Lane, Robert. 1959. *Political Life: Why People Get Involved*. Illinois: The Free Press.

Langston, Kenneth, and Ronald Rapoport. 1975. "Social Structure, Social Context and Partisan Mobilization." *Comparative Political Studies*. 8:318–344.

Lemann, Nicholas.1986a. "The Origins of the Underclass." *The Atlantic Monthly*, 257 (June 1986).

———. 1986b. "The Origins of the Underclass." *The Atlantic Monthly*. 258 (July 1986).

———. 1991. *The Promised Land*. New York: Alfred Knopf.

Lipset, Seymour Martin. 1960. *Political Man*. New York: Doubleday.

Loury, Glen. 1985. "The Moral Quandary of the Black Community." *The Public Interest*. 79:9–22.

MacKuen, Michael, and Courtney Brown. 1987. "Political Context and Attitude Change." *American Political Science Review*. 81:471–90.

Mansbridge, Jane. 1990. "The Rise and Fall of Self-Interest in Explanation of Political Life," *Beyond Self-Interest*, Jane Mansbridge, editor. Chicago: University of Chicago Press.

Mare, Robert D., and Christopher Winship. 1991. "Socioeconomic Change and the Decline of Marriage for Blacks and Whites," *The Urban Underclass*. Paul Peterson and Christopher Jencks, editors. Washington, D.C.: The Brookings Institution

Marsden, Peter V. 1987. "Core Discussion Networks of Americans." *American Sociological Review*. 52:122–31.

Massey, Douglas, and Nancy A. Denton. 1993. *American Apartheid*. Cambridge: Harvard University Press.

Martin, William. 1996. *With God on Our Side*. New York: Broadway Books.

Mayer, Susan E. 1991. "How Much Does a High School's Racial and Socioeconomic Mix Affect Graduation and Teenage Fertility Rates?" *The Urban Underclass*, Christopher Jencks and Paul Peterson, editors. Washington, D.C.: The Brookings Institution.

Mayhew, David. 1974. *Congress: The Electoral Connection*. New Haven: Yale University Press.

McLanahan, Sara. 1995. "Family Structure and the Reproduction of Poverty." *American Journal of Sociology*. 90:873–901.

———, and Irwin Garfinkel. 1989. "Single Mothers, the Underclass and Social Policy." *The Annals of the American Academy*. 501(2):92–104.

————, and Gary Sandefur. 1994. *Growing Up with a Single Parent: What Hurts, What Helps*. Cambridge: Harvard University Press.

McPhee, William. 1963. "A Theory of Informal Social Influence," *Formal Theories of Mass Behavior*, William N. McPhee, editor. New York: Free Press.

Mead, Lawrence. 1986. *Beyond Entitlement*. New York: Free Press.

————. 1992. *The New Politics of Poverty*. New York: Basic Books.

Milbrath, Lester. 1965. *Political Participation: How and Why Do People Get Involved in Politics?* Chicago: Rand, McNally and Co.

Mincy, Ronald B. 1988. "Underclass Variation by Race and Place: Have Large Cities Darkened Our Picture of the Underclass?" Working paper, The Urban Institute, Washington, D.C.

————, Isabell Sawhill and Douglass Wolf. 1990. "The Underclass: Definition and Measurement." *Science*. 248:450–453.

————, and Samuel Wiener. 1995. "Concentrated Poverty and the Underclass." *Two Views of Urban America* (Rockefeller Institute Bulletin).

Moffit, Robert. 1994. "Welfare Effects on Female Headship with Area Effects." *Journal of Human Resources*. 29(2):621–637.

Morris, Aldon. 1984. *The Origins of the Civil Rights Movement: Black Communities Organizing for Change*. New York: Free Press.

Morris, David, and Karl Hess. 1975. *Neighborhood Power: The New Localism*. New York: Beacon Press.

Moynihan, Daniel Patrick. 1965. *The Negro Family: The Case for National Action*. Washington, D.C.: Office of Policy Planning and Research, U.S. Department of Labor.

Muller, Thomas. 1993. *Immigrants and the American City*. New York: New York University Press.

Murray, Charles. 1984. *Losing Ground*. New York: Basic Books Inc.

————. 1993. "The Coming White Underclass." *The Wall Street Journal*, October 29 .

Myrdal, Gunnar. 1963. *An American Dilemma*. New York: Harper and Row.

Nagel, Jack H. 1987. *Participation*. Englewood Cliffs, NJ: Prentice-Hall.

Nelson, Barbara. 1984. "Women's Poverty and Women's Citizenship: Some Political Consequences of Economic Marginality," *Women and Poverty*, Barbara C. Gelpi, editor. Chicago: University of Chicago Press.

Obershall, Anthony. 1973. *Social Conflict and Social Movements*. Englewood Cliffs, NJ: Prentice-Hall.

Olsen, Marvin. 1970. "Social and Political Participation of Blacks." *American Sociological Review*. 35:682–697.

Olson, Mancur. 1965. *The Logic of Collective Action*. Cambridge: Harvard University Press.

Opp, Karl-Dieter. 1986. "Soft Incentives and Collective Action." *British Journal of Political Science*. 16:86–112.

Orfield, Gary, and Carole Ashkinaze. 1991. *The Closing Door*. Chicago: University of Chicago Press.

Orum, Anthony M. 1966. "A Reappraisal of the Social and Political Participation of Negroes." *American Journal of Sociology*. 72:32–46.

Osterman, Paul. 1991. "Gains from Growth: The Impact of Full Employment on Poverty in Boston,"*The Urban Underclass*, Christopher Jencks and Paul Peterson, editors. Washington, D.C.: Brookings Institution.

Ostrum, Elinor. 1976. *The Delivery of Urban Services: Outcomes of Change*. Beverly Hills: Sage Publications.

Overbea, Luix. 1986. "Secession Scare Has Boston Mayor Mending Fences with Blacks," *The Christian Science Monitor*, November 20, p. 9.

Pear, Robert. 1993. "Poverty 1993: Bigger, Deeper, Getting Worse." *New York Times*, October 10, E5.

Peterson, Paul. 1990. *Welfare Magnets*. Washington, D.C.: Brookings Institution.

Piven, Frances Fox and Richard Cloward. 1977. *Poor People's Movements: Why They Succeed, How They Fail*. New York: Vintage Books.

———. 1984. *The New Class War: Reagan's Attacks on the Welfare State and Its Consequences*. New York: Pantheon Books.

———. 1987. *Why Americans Don't Vote*. New York:Pantheon Books.

Putnam, Robert C., with Robert Leonardi and Raffaella Y. Nanetti. 1993. *Making Democracy Work: Civic Traditions in Modern Italy*. Princeton: Princeton University Press.

———. 1995. "Bowling Alone." *Journal of Democracy*. January:76.

Quadagno, Jill. 1994. *The Color of Welfare*. New York: Oxford University Press.

Randall, Vicky. 1987. *Women and Politics: An International Perspective*. Chicago: University of Chicago Press.

Reed, Adolph, Jr. 1991. "The Underclass as Myth and Symbol: The Poverty of Discourse About Poverty." *Radical America* 24(1): 1–3.

Riker, William H. and Peter C. Ordeshook. 1968. "A Theory of the Calculus of Voting." *American Political Science Review*. 62:25–42.

Ricketts, Erroll, and Isabell Sawhill. 1988. "Defining and Measuring the Underclass." *Journal of Policy Analysis and Management*. 7:316–325.

Rinehart, Sue Tolleson. 1992. *Gender Consciousness and Politics*. New York: Routledge, Chapman and Hall.

Rose, Harold and Paula McClain. 1990. *Race, Place and Risk: Black Homicide in Urban America*. Albany: State University of New York Press.

Rosenstone, Steven, and John Hansen. 1993. *Mobilization, Participation and Democracy in America*. New York: Macmillan Publishing Company.

Rovener, Julie, with Kitty Duman, Susan Kellam and Jill Zuckman. 1992. "Rhetoric, Not Radical Change Likely Result of L.A. Riots." *Congressional Quarterly*, May 9, pp. 1247–1255.

Rusk, David. 1993. *Cities Without Suburbs*. Baltimore: Woodrow Wilson Center Press, distributed by Johns Hopkins University.

Sampson, Robert J. 1987. "Urban Black Violence:The Effects of Male Joblessness and Family Disruption." *American Journal of Sociology*. 93(2):348–82.

Schlozman, Kay, Nancy Burns, and Sidney Verba. 1994. "Gender and the Pathways to Participation: The Role of Resources." *Journal of Politics*. 56(4):963–990.

Schlozman, Kay, Nancy Burns, Sidney Verba, and Jesse Donahue. 1995. "Gender and Citizen Participation: Is There a Different Voice?" *American Journal of Political Science*. 39:267–294.

Schwarz, John E. 1985. "Murray's Mistake." *The New Leader*. 68:3–5.

Segal, David, and M. Meyer. 1969. "Social Context and Individual Behavior," *Quantitative Ecological Analysis in the Social Sciences*, M. Dogan and S. Rokkan, editors, Cambridge: MIT Press.

Shultz, Paul. 1994. "Marital Status and Fertility in the United States: Welfare and Labor Market Effects." *Journal of Human Resources*. 29(2):637–39.

Skocpol, Theda. 1991. "Targeting Within Universalism." *The Urban Underclass*, Christopher Jencks and Paul E. Peterson, editors. Washington, D.C.: Brookings Institution.

Sniderman, Paul M. and Thomas Piazza. 1993. *The Scar of Race*. Cambridge: Harvard University Press.

Squires, Gregory. 1994. *Capital and Communities in Black And White*. Albany: State University of New York.

Stack, Carol B. 1974. *All Our Kin: Strategies for Survival In A Black Community*. New York: Harper and Row.

Stoker, Laura, and M. Kent Jennings. 1995. "Life-Cycle and Political Participation: The Case of Marriage." *American Political Science Association*. 89(2):421–436.

Stone, Clarence. 1987. *Regime Politics: Governing Atlanta, 1946–1988*. Lawrence, KS: University Press of Kansas.

Straits, Bruce C. 1991. "Bringing Strong Ties Back in: Interpersonal Gateways to Political Information and Influence." *Public Opinion Quarterly.* 55:432–88.

Sullivan, Mercer. 1989. "Absent Father in the Inner City." *The Annals.* 501(2):26–47.

Swanstrom, Todd. 1985. *The Crisis of Growth Politics.* Philadelphia: Temple University Press.

Tate, Katherine. 1993. *From Protest to Politics.* Cambridge and New York: Harvard University Press and Russell Sage Foundation.

Tienda, Marta, and Haya Stier. 1991. "Joblessness and Shiftlessness: Labor Force Activity in Chicago's Inner City," *The Urban Underclass,* Christopher Jencks and Paul Peterson, editors. Washington, D.C.: Brookings Institution.

Urban Land Institute. 1992. "An Evaluation of Citywide Delivery System for Affordable Housing and of Revitalizing Strategies for the Hilltop, Mt. Vernon and South Linden Neighborhoods." Report Prepared for the City of Columbus, Ohio.

Van Haitsma, Martha. 1990. "A Contextual Definition of the Underclass." *Focus.* (12):27–31.

Verba, Sidney, Kay Lehman Schlozman, Henry Brady and Norman Nie. 1993. "Citizen Activity: Who Participates? What Do They Say?" *American Political Science Review.* 87(2):303–318.

———, and Norman Nie. 1972. *Political Participation in America.* New York: Harper and Row.

———, Kay Lehman Schlozman and Henry Brady. 1995. *Voice and Equality.* Cambridge: Harvard University Press.

Wacquant, Loïc. 1996. The Comparative Structure and Experience of Urban Exclusion: 'Race,' Class and Space in Chicago and Paris," *Poverty, Inequality, and the Future of Social Policy,* Katherine McFate, Roger Lawson, and William Julius Wilson, editors. New York: Russell Sage Foundation.

Wald, Kenneth. 1987. *Religion and Politics in the United States.* New York: St. Martin's Press.

———, Dennis E. Owen, and Samuel S. Hill, Jr. 1988. "Churches as Political Communities." *American Political Science Review.* 28:531–547.

Walton, Hanes, Jr. 1985. *Invisible Politics.* Albany: State University of New York Press.

———. 1988. *When the Marching Stopped: The Politics of Civil Rights Regulatory Agencies.* Albany: State University of New York Press.

————. 1994. *Black Politics and Black Political Behavior*. Westport, CT: Greenwood.

Ware, Jane. 1991. "Franklinton, Eldest of All." *Columbus Monthly*, pp. 10–11.

Warren, Robert. 1995. "National Urban Policy and the Local State: Paradoxes of Meaning, Action and Consequences," *Exploring Urban America*, Roger W. Caves, editor. Thousand Oaks: Sage.

Welch, Susan. 1977. "Women as Political Animals? A Test of Some Explanations for Male-Female Political Differences." *American Journal of Political Science*. 21:711–30.

Williams, Walter. 1996. "The Welfare Debate." *Society*. 33(5):13–15.

Wilson, William J. 1980. *The Declining Significance of Race*. Chicago: University of Chicago Press.

————. 1987. *The Truly Disadvantaged*. Chicago: University of Chicago Press.

————. 1996. *When Work Disappears*. New York: Knopf.

————, and Loïc J.D. Wacquant. 1989. "The Cost of Racial and Class Exclusion in the Inner-City." *The Annals*. 501:(22):8–25.

Wolfinger, Raymond, and Steven Rosenstone. 1980. *Who Votes?* New Haven: Yale University Press.

Wright, Gerald. 1976. "Community Structure and Voting in the South." *Public Opinion Quarterly*. 40:200–15.

————. 1977. "Contextual Models of Electoral Behavior: The Southern Wallace Vote." *American Political Science Review*. 71:497–508.

Index